Family Entrepreneurship in Emerging Markets

In this fascinating study, Neri Karra examines entrepreneurial family businesses in emerging markets by integrating three schools of thought: agency theory, an institutional framework, and the altruism perspective.

Providing an in-depth treatment of the area as well as a real-life case study, it provides a theoretical perspective as well as qualitative insights. It also offers practical observations and future research implications.

This book will be valuable reading to students and researchers of entrepreneurship, family businesses, and altruism in management.

Neri Karra is an Associate Professor in Entrepreneurship at IÉSEG University in France. She is also the founder of the Neri Karra luxury fashion brand.

Family Entrepreneurship in Emerging Markets

Neri Karra

Routledge
Taylor & Francis Group

LONDON AND NEW YORK

First published 2018
by Routledge
2 Park Square, Milton Park, Abingdon, Oxon OX14 4RN

and by Routledge
711 Third Avenue, New York, NY 10017

Routledge is an imprint of the Taylor & Francis Group, an informa business

© 2018 Neri Karra

British Library Cataloguing-in-Publication Data
A catalogue record for this book is available from the British Library

Library of Congress Cataloging-in-Publication Data
Names: Karra, Neri, author.
Title: Family entrepreneurship in emerging markets /
Neri Karra.
Description: 1 Edition. | New York: Routledge, 2018. |
Includes bibliographical references and index.
Identifiers: LCCN 2017021110 (print) | LCCN 2017022311
(ebook) | ISBN 9781315164410 (eBook) | ISBN 9781138058231
(hardback: alk. paper)
Subjects: LCSH: Family-owned business enterprises—
Developing countries. | Entrepreneurship—Developing
countries.
Classification: LCC HD62.25 (ebook) | LCC HD62.25 .K37
2018 (print) | DDC 338/.04091724—dc23
LC record available at https://lccn.loc.gov/2017021110

ISBN: 978-1-138-05823-1 (hbk)
ISBN: 978-1-315-16441-0 (ebk)

Typeset in Times New Roman
by codeMantra

For my parents, Halide and Ismail—with my deepest gratitude.

Contents

Illustrations

Figures

Tables

Foreword

Family businesses are considered the backbone of the economy in almost all countries. Family businesses tend to have their own unique composition compared to other businesses; this also leads them to face complex challenges: in business and investment, but also ownership issues and family dynamics and relationships. Both anecdotal and academic knowledge tells us that most family-owned companies tend to struggle to survive beyond a single generation. Family businesses tend to be especially vulnerable at times of transition in leadership, where there is often a conflict between the desire to maintain tradition and the need to adapt to the changing environment of a business. Emerging market economies add a particular challenge to this already complicated picture, since these economies are characterized by instability, constant change, and the need to not only respect tradition within a larger context but also possess agility to adapt to the demands of the rapidly changing worldwide economy.

I started my PhD while building a family business that operated mainly in emerging market economies that were faced with sudden political disruption: Turkey, Russia, and the former Soviet Republics. Communism just ended, which created its own unique challenges as well as opportunities, while Turkey was becoming the bridge to newly budding entrepreneurs in its own market as well as to those from the former communist regime, who now could become entrepreneurs. Most of these businesses took shape as family businesses and grew from small sized business to holding companies operating in multiple markets. Our own family business was created in the late 1990s, in an environment that could only be characterized as highly unique, which offered me the chance to examine it while completing my Doctoral thesis. What started as a personal interest would turn into an academic curiosity, followed by presentations in academic conferences, research seminars, and eventually publication.

The book consists of a collection of research papers and essays that tell the story of my own family business, while interlinking the dynamics of a family business in an emerging market economy. The book aims to guide the reader to an understanding of what it takes to create a successful family business in such an environment, details the necessary success factors and dynamics, and provides an understanding of the institutional environment and how an entrepreneur could act as a bridge between two completely different institutional contexts.

The book is unique as it provides an in-depth look of a family-owned firm that operated in a highly unique context, geographically, politically, and economically.

Acknowledgment

Nobody ever does anything alone, and while this book may have my name as the author, it has been the result of almost a decade of work that started with my Doctoral thesis at University of Cambridge. Therefore, I would like to thank my academic supervisor, Dr. Simon Bell, and my colleagues and co-authors Professor Nelson Phillips and Professor Paul Tracey for their guidance and support.

I would like to thank Professor Tamer Cavusgil, who believed in me from the very beginning and encouraged the publication of this book, as well as my previous one. Professor Jonathan Pinto has guided me with his knowledge, as well as good humour, while completing this book.

Versions of these papers have been presented at workshops and seminars at the University of Calgary, University of Cambridge, and McGill University as well as at the meetings of the Academy of Management. I am deeply grateful for all the guidance that was shared during these meetings, which has shaped the final version of my publications.

Finally, I would like to thank my family—my parents and my brother, especially—for their unwavering support and for instilling me with values that have allowed me to do work with great love. I am immensely grateful that I get to do what I love, and this to me has been the biggest gift in this lifetime. Thank you!

1 Introduction

In emerging economies, roughly 60 percent of private-sector companies with revenues of $1 billion or more were family owned in 2010 (Bjornberg, Elstrodt, and Pandit, 2014). A McKinsey survey of 60 leading family-owned companies in Asia, South America, and Central America showed their "organizational health" to be equal to or better than other companies in the same markets (Bjornberg, Elstrodt, and Pandit, 2014).

Despite the importance and significance of family business, however, management scholars have devoted little attention to this topic overall (Lumpkin, Steir and Wright, 2011) and have mainly focused on family firms in developed economies. Moreover, theories in the family business literature are often based on particular points of view (e.g., Anglo-American) and tested in developed economies. This limits our understanding of family firms around the world as the contexts of where they have been founded, developed, and operated may differ substantially. Therefore, the validity, reliability, and applicability of existing theories may be questioned.

Recent studies have attempted to resolve this issue by focusing on culture in terms of its effects on family entrepreneurial behavior and family firm heterogeneity, (e.g., Discua Cruz and Howorth, 2008; Gupta and Levenburg, 2010; Rosa et al., 2014) and by relating family firms and their geographical context (Basco, 2015). In spite of this research, however, we still know little about family businesses in developing, emerging, and transitional economies.

This book begins to fill this gap by focusing on a company with a network in developing countries. Chapter 2 portrays a family-owned firm headquartered in Istanbul—Neroli. Founded in 1990, at the time of this writing, Neroli had already grown into a medium-sized company selling leather goods and clothing. It had a distribution network that included Russia, many of the former Soviet republics, and Eastern Europe.

In Chapter 2, we'll explore how this firm was started and the forces that propelled its rapid growth. Specifically, employing Neroli as an example, I'll focus on agency theory and altruism as it relates to family business. Along the way, I'll answer some key questions. For example, it's generally accepted that altruism is a prime feature of family businesses—one that differentiates them from non-family firms. But how is it that altruism can be a double-edged sword—decreasing agency costs in some instances and increasing them in others? We'll look closely at the circumstances that create this dichotomy.

Then there are more questions. First, can altruism be successfully extended beyond the biological family to what I call a *quasi-family* based on kinship and ethnicity? Will the members of this quasi-family reciprocate in kind—and will these altruistic behaviors reduce agency problems?

Neroli also figures prominently in Chapter 3. But while Chapter 2 discusses the firm mainly in the context of the immediate family, Chapter 3 expands this discussion to focus on the role of ethnicity. We'll observe how Neroli created a successful international network of businesses based on the ethnicity of its various members.

We'll begin with an overview of ethnic businesses formed by immigrants. Because immigrants may have difficulty with the language and customs of their adopted country, the businesses they form tend to market to and employ members of their own ethnic group. As they grow, however, some of these firms may expand into the larger economy of their new country or even go international by leveraging ties with their home country. Neroli is a prime example of a small ethnic firm that grew large by marketing its products internationally.

The literature on ethnic entrepreneurship, however, has not yet caught up with companies like Neroli, tending instead to focus on the more traditional small firms that serve their own ethnic populations. This leads us to pose two questions: First, what role do ethnic networks play in helping non-traditional small firms grow large? Second, how well does the existing literature explain this role?

Other questions in this chapter relate to the advantages and disadvantages of networks based on kinship and ethnicity. What are the favorable aspects of such networks? What are the downsides, and can they be rectified? How is it that the ties in Neroli's broad ethnic network enabled its rapid growth in the early years but came to limit growth in later years? You will find answers to these questions and more as the story of Neroli's rapid expansion into Russia and Eastern Europe unfolds.

In Chapter 4, we will focus on how entrepreneurs in emerging markets can create value by solving institutional problems. In developed economies, the rules, regulations, customs, and procedures governing business activities are taken for granted. In many emerging markets, however, these institutions are minimal and/or low functioning, and for many businesses, this acts as a barrier to entrepreneurship.

The question here is: How can creative and risk-tolerant entrepreneurs transform this institutional uncertainty into exciting opportunities? I will focus in particular on how entrepreneurs in emerging markets can act as "institutional entrepreneurs" and create value by solving institutional problems.

I'll introduce neo-institutional theory as a useful framework for observing emerging market economies. Because neo-institutional theory focuses on both formal and informal institutional processes and the role of actors in shaping institutional change, I consider it to be a good foundation for research in emerging markets.

In Chapter 2 we will discuss altruism and agency in the family firm and explore the role of family, kinship, and ethnicity.

References

Basco, R. (2015). Family Business and Regional Development. A theoretical model of regional familiness. *Journal of Family Business Strategy*, No. Forthcoming.

Bjornberg, A., Elstrodt, H.-P., and Pandit, V. (2014). The family-business factor in emerging markets. *McKinsey Quarterly*, December, pp. 1–6.

Discua Cruz, A. & Howorth, C. (2008). Family business in Honduras: Applicability of agency and stewardship theories. In Gupta, V., Levenburg, N., Moore, L., Motwani, J. and Schwarz, T. (eds.), *Culturally-sensitive models of family business in Latin America.* Hyderabad: ICFAI University Press, pp. 222–243.

Gupta, V. & Levenburg, N. (2010). A thematic analysis of cultural variations in family businesses: The CASE project. *Family Business Review*, 23(2), 155–169.

Lumpkin, G., Steier, L., & Wright, M. (2011). Strategic entrepreneurship in family business. *Strategic Entrepreneurship Journal*, 5(4), 285–306.

Rosa, P., Howorth, C., & Discua Cruz, A. (2014). Habitual and portfolio entrepreneurship and the family in business. In Melin, L., Nordqvist, M. and Sharma, P. (eds.), *The SAGE family business handbook*. Sage: London.

2 Altruism and agency in the family firm
Exploring the role of family, kinship, and ethnicity

This chapter examines the relationship between altruism and agency costs in family business through an in-depth case study of a family firm. This study found that while altruism reduced agency costs in the early stages of the business, agency costs increased as the venture became larger and more established. In addition, the study suggests that altruistic behavior may not be confined to family and close kin, but may rather extend through networks of distant kin and ethnic ties. All this presents a more complex view of the agency relationship in family business than is usually portrayed in the existing literature.

Chrisman, Chua, and Sharma (2005: 559) suggest that the core challenge facing family business research is to identify "the nature of family firms' distinctions" and to determine "if and how these distinctions result from family involvement." As family business researchers have grappled with these issues, they have relied heavily on agency theory and in particular on the notion of altruism. While this approach has resulted in a number of important insights, the effects of altruism in family business still remain uncertain. For example, it is unclear what conditions cause altruism to reduce agency costs (e.g., Van Den Berghe and Carchon, 2003) and what conditions cause altruism to increase them (e.g., Schulze, Lubatkin, and Dino, 2003).

This lack of clarity suggests that considerably more work is required to develop a comprehensive theory of altruism as a distinctive aspect of family business. Moreover, even though altruism may affect the non-family members of family firms, this issue has rarely been examined in the literature. The case study of a family business presented in this chapter grew out of a larger research project I conducted from 2002 to 2005 (2005) and sheds significant light on this topic. This larger study looked at new entrepreneurial ventures that began international operations soon after their founding. During this research project, it became apparent that many of these companies were family owned and possessed complex networks of family, kinship, and ethnic ties.

I then selected one firm from this larger study to explore the family dynamics that occurred in the development of these ventures. The firm that was chosen, Neroli,[1] is a medium-sized fashion firm headquartered in Turkey that manufactures and sells a range of leather goods and clothing. It has production facilities in Istanbul and a distribution network spanning much of the former Soviet Union and Eastern Europe.

By exploring the role of family influence in the development of this family-owned new venture, this study makes several contributions to the family business literature. First, the study demonstrates that in the early stages of family businesses, altruistic behavior has the potential to align the interests of family and kin and help build competitive advantage.

Second, the research illustrates how family firms may expand the family model beyond the nuclear family; by including kinship and ethnicity, a kind of *quasi-family* may be created. In this case, the owner of Neroli leveraged ethnic ties and the shared experience of living under communism to build a network of relationships that shared the characteristics of the family ties at the center of the firm. This suggests a more fluid conception of "family"—one that is at least partly negotiated rather than automatically attributed by virtue of blood or marriage.

Third, the study shows that there are limits to altruism as family businesses develop and grow, and that agency costs may, therefore, increase over time. However, I found that the nature of the agency problems are different for the family and near kin as opposed to the quasi-family based on distant kin and ethnic ties. With regard to the former, agency issues take the form of moral hazard; in the latter, they take the form of adverse selection.

This chapter proceeds as follows: First, there is an overview of the literature on agency theory and altruism as it relates to family business. Next, the research questions that underpin the study are outlined. I will then explain why I chose Neroli and how the data were collected and analyzed. In the third section, we will look at the story of Neroli. Building on the case study, in the fourth section I'll present my findings on the relationship between altruism and agency in family firms. Finally, we'll consider the implications of the study and discuss some directions for future research.

Agency theory, altruism, and the family firm

There is a large and growing body of work that considers the ways in which family businesses differ from non-family businesses (Chrisman et al., 2005). One of the most successful approaches to developing a theory of the family firm has been the agency theory. This theory takes into account the distinctive dynamics of the family business and the role of the business as a family institution. At the core of agency theory is the potential conflict between the owners of a firm (the principal) and the managers under contract to run the firm on the owners' behalf (the agent).

Agency theory highlights two characteristics of agency relationships (Eisenhardt, 1989a): (1) the interests and objectives of both the agent and the principal and (2) the approach to risk of the agent and the principal. Both the interests and the approach to risk are likely to diverge under certain circumstances, and this may lead to conflicting decisions. Because of asymmetric information, it can be difficult for the principal to monitor the actions of the agent. Moreover, because contracts are incomplete—that is, unable to address all possible contingencies—it's impossible for the principal to ensure that the agent acts appropriately in all circumstances (Alchian and Woodward, 1988).

Because of asymmetric information and the absence of complete contracts, two kinds of agency problem may arise (Chrisman, Chua, and Litz, 2004). The first is adverse selection, which occurs when the principal enters into a contract with an agent who is not well qualified or is unsuitable for the tasks to be performed. The second is moral hazard, a term that "suggests that people cannot be counted on to do what they say they are going to do, and that failure manifests itself in prices and contractual arrangements" (Alchian and Woodward, 1988: 68). Moral hazard is a form of opportunism and includes shirking, free riding, and the overconsumption of perks.

Agency problems such as these can hinder cooperative relationships between agents and principals. To control these problems, principals may adopt a series of incentive mechanisms (both hortatory and punitive) to try to ensure that the actions of the agent are consistent with the objectives of the principal. The costs of negotiating and implementing these incentives, as well as the costs of monitoring them, are referred to as agency costs.

Early proponents of agency theory suggested that agency costs in family firms are negligible or absent, because the interests of family members are likely to be closely aligned (Fama and Jensen, 1983, 1985). They argue that this leads to effective decision making because owners have the capacity to ensure that decisions are made with a view to maximizing family wealth and/or securing a legacy for future generations. Jensen and Meckling (1976) even suggested that formal governance mechanisms in family firms are at best unnecessary and at worst actually damaging for business performance. From this perspective, family business is a very efficient form of organization, with

Agency theory brings to mind the challenges facing many publicly owned corporations today. Imagine that shareholders of Company B (the *principal*) hire a new CEO (*agent*) to grow the company and improve shareholder value. As an incentive, they make a large part of the CEO's compensation dependent on the price of the stock (this is an *agency cost*).

Now, the new CEO is very knowledgeable in Company B's specialty, which is a certain kind of software. She can see that the only way for the company to survive and prosper is to aim for long-term success. This means allocating for a generous research budget and retaining skilled employees.

The shareholders are not happy with this plan, however. They advocate for measures that would raise the price of the stock immediately. These include spending the research money on a stock-repurchase program and firing 20 percent of the employees. Because the shareholders don't have the knowledge and information of the CEO (*asymmetric information*)—or simply because they're aiming for short-term gain—their interests differ from those of the CEO.

Activist shareholders, like those of Company B, represent a major challenge for US corporations in the twenty-first century. Many corporations would like to plan for the long term but find that large numbers of their shareholders simply want policies that grow the stock price in the short term.

Small, family-owned firms may not have exactly the same challenges because the agent and the principal are usually the same people. In fact, family-owned firms are known for their ability to plan for the long term (Bjornberg, Elstrodt, and Pandit, 2014).

intrinsic advantages over non-family organizational forms (Daily and Dollinger, 1992; Kang, 2000).

The assumption of these authors is that individuals, households, and firms are rational actors seeking to maximize their economic utility. In more recent family business studies, however, comparatively few scholars have sought to work within these confines, preferring instead to consider that actors may have a range of preferences and objectives (e.g., Chrisman et al., 2004; Lubatkin, Schulze, Ling, and Dino, 2005). More specifically, a key assumption in the family business literature is that in addition to economic goals, families may have certain non-economic goals such as providing employment for family members and building family cohesion.[2] This changes the nature of the agency relationship because it is possible for family members to make decisions that lead to suboptimal business performance—for example, by the excessive consumption of perks—but at the same time exhibit behaviors that are consistent with the objectives of the owner of the firm (Chrisman et al., 2004).

In seeking to explain this characteristic of family firms, the concept of *altruism* figures prominently. Van den Berghe and Carchon (2003) suggest that altruism provides a powerful conceptual tool for understanding why family firms exist. Dyer (2003: 408) voices a similar opinion, arguing that it plays "a unique role in family firms that is not generally found in other enterprises."

In religious studies, and in some strands of philosophy, altruism refers to a moral value that leads individuals to act in the interests of others without the expectation of reward or positive reinforcement in return. In economics, on the other hand, altruism is considered a utility function that connects the welfare of one individual to that of others (Schulze et al., 2003); for the most part, this conception of altruism has been applied in family business studies. Thus, parents may exhibit high levels of munificence with respect to their children, not only because of the bond that exists between them, but also because their own interests, and those of the business, might be damaged were they to act less benevolently.

There is much debate about whether altruistic behavior increases and/or decreases agency costs in family firms. Van den Berghe and Carchon (2003), for example, argue that altruism encourages a number of behaviors that reduce agency costs and improve firm performance. First, altruistic behavior creates a self-reinforcing system of incentives that encourages family members to be thoughtful and "selfless" toward one another. Second, it gives rise to a sense of collective ownership amongst the family members employed in the firm. Third, it reduces the information asymmetries among family members. Finally, it generates an organizational culture that encourages risk-taking—for example, exploring international growth opportunities (Zahra, 2003).

There is some empirical evidence to support this position, especially when the altruism is reciprocal and symmetrical (i.e., exhibited evenly by both parties). For example, Chrisman et al. (2004) found that, overall, family involvement may decrease agency problems, and Eaton, Yuang, and Wu (2002) show econometrically that reciprocal and symmetrical altruism leads to competitive advantages with respect to some business opportunities.[3] Chua and Schnabel (1986), Chami (1997), and Carney (2005) also provide evidence to suggest that altruism can help build competitive advantage.

However, there is empirical evidence to suggest that altruism may be a "two-edged sword" (Dyer, 2003: 405). For example, Schulze et al. (2003: 475) noted that "altruism compels parents to care for their children, encourages family members to be considerate of one another, and makes family membership valuable in ways that both promote and sustain the bond among them." However, they also found a number of important agency problems closely associated with altruism. These include free riding, biased views from parents about the capabilities of their children, the overconsumption of perks by family members, and problems in the enforcement of contracts. This led them to conclude that "family-ownership does not appear to represent the kind of governance panacea that Fama and Jensen (1983) and others attribute to family owner-management" (Schulze et al., 2003: 487). Building on this work, Lubatkin et al. (2005) also demonstrate empirically that there may be a "darker side" to altruism in family business. In the same vein, Gomez-Mejia, Nunez-Nickel, and Gutierrez (2001) show that the preferential treatment of family members leads to increased rather than decreased problems of agency.

It's evident that we have a mixed picture here. We have relatively limited empirical evidence, and the empirical evidence that does exist suggests that altruism may have both positive and negative implications for the principal-agent relationship. This leaves us with important questions about the effects of altruistic behavior on agency costs in the family firm. The most critical question is: Under what circumstances does altruism increase and/or reduce agency costs? Rephrased as a research question, it reads like this:

What is the relationship between altruism and agency costs in family businesses? Does this relationship vary over time?

The rest of the chapter addresses these questions through an in-depth case study of a successful family business. This case is particularly interesting, not only because altruism formed a central strand of the founder's strategy from the firm's inception, but also because the altruistic behavior he exhibited was directed toward both family members *and* key non-family members of the business and its network. Moreover, unlike much of the existing empirical evidence, which is predominantly quantitative in nature, the use of qualitative methods allowed agency issues to be explored in a way that includes the context in which the focal firm operated. This enabled the research to track the evolving relationship between altruism and agency costs over a period spanning several years.

Methodology

As noted, the study that forms the basis of this article began in 2002 when I interviewed the owner and CEO of Neroli, Ishmael Karov, as part of a larger research project on international new venture creation (Karra, 2005). Karov founded Neroli in Istanbul in the late-1990s and guided it through a period of rapid growth, successfully penetrating markets across Eastern Europe. By the end of the study, the firm employed about 750 people and had 87 retail outlets across the former Soviet Republics and Eastern Europe.

I chose to study Neroli for three reasons. First, the case has "rare or unique" qualities that make it a logical candidate for "theoretical sampling" (Eisenhardt, 1989b; Yin, 1994). Preliminary research revealed that the firm had grown rapidly over a relatively short period and relied upon a high level of family involvement. The organization of the firm remained family based, and most employees were relatives or shared the same ethnic background as the owner. In addition, the entrepreneur's motivation for founding the firm was the betterment of the family; the dynamics of the family were, therefore, central to the firm.

Second, Karov provided a very high level of access to the firm. Not only was I able to interview him and other important members of the firm on multiple occasions during the period of the study, he also provided me with extensive archival data relating to the history of the firm. In addition, I was able to travel with him to attend key meetings with distributors and retailers in Russia and Eastern Europe and to attend trade shows and visit important suppliers in Italy. I was also able to interview all family members and other key individuals including manufacturing partners and employees.

Third, the firm was only slightly more than a decade old at the time of the study, and the founder was still the CEO of the company. This was significant because it increased the likelihood that the details of the founding of the firm and its early development remained fresh in the minds of the founder and other interviewees. Therefore, I consider Neroli a "strategic research site" (Bijker, Hughes, and Pinch, 1987) for studying altruism in family business.

Data collection and analysis

I collected archival data and conducted interviews during several trips to Istanbul and during visits to Russia, Ukraine, Kazakhstan, and Azerbaijan. In addition, I conducted a number of telephone interviews with key members of the firm and its partners in Turkey, Italy, the United States, and the former Soviet Republics. Because I speak English, Turkish, Russian, Italian, and Bulgarian, I was able to conduct many of the interviews in the first language of the interviewees. Substantial secondary data was collected in order to understand the historical context within which the firm was founded.

The data were analyzed in a two-stage process. In the first stage, the case study was organized into an "event history database" (Garud and Rappa, 1994). This was done by chronologically ordering descriptions of events taken from the raw data like interview transcripts, interview and field notes, and secondary sources such as journalists' accounts of the political and economic context. These multiple accounts were then juxtaposed against each other to ascertain the degree of convergence. Because I had previously worked for the company as a translator from 1996 to 2002, I had a detailed understanding of the growth of the firm.[4] This knowledge, combined with the interview and field notes, allowed for the development of a detailed narrative of the formation and subsequent expansion of the firm (See Table 2.1).

In the second stage of data analysis, I documented and tracked the motivations of the entrepreneur, the degree of involvement of family members, the role of other key actors, the evolving business model, and the factors that emerged as critical to the firm's success. I then examined the evolution of the firm over time, paying particular attention to the role of family members and evidence of altruism and agency costs. As I developed the chronology of the case, I carefully documented the theoretical issues that emerged. In this last process of "enfolding findings with the literature" (Eisenhardt, 1989b), I brought together, iteratively, findings from my research on the company—Neroli—and related them to the literature on family business and to the research questions. During this process I moved back and forth between data and theory until we reached "theoretical saturation" (Garud, Sanjay, and Arun, 2002).

Let's now take a look at our focal company, Neroli—its story and the context in which it was founded.

Neroli: a family-owned international new venture

Ishmael Karov and his family were among 360,000 Turkish Bulgarians forced to emigrate from Bulgaria to Turkey in June 1989. Following their emigration, Karov and his brothers found work as welders in Istanbul, while their wives worked as cleaners and textile workers. Very soon, however, frustrated with the lack of opportunities for immigrants in his new country, Karov concluded that "working in factories, for someone else's profit, would never do the family any good." In order to raise capital for a business, he went back to Bulgaria and sold the family property.

Karov's idea was to open up a store in Laleli, a neighborhood in Istanbul frequented by non-Turkish entrepreneurs known as "luggage traders." Following the collapse of the Berlin wall, there was an insatiable demand for consumer goods in former Communist countries. Responding to this demand, thousands of entrepreneurs from the newly capitalist transition economies of Eastern Europe and the former Soviet Union began to visit Istanbul. These entrepreneurs came to the city to buy inexpensive Turkish merchandise, which they then took back to their home countries "in their luggage" for resale. These luggage traders provided an unexpected, but very welcome, export opportunity for shrewd entrepreneurs. Although largely unofficial, this trade reached an estimated US$8.8 billion by 1998, a significant proportion of Turkey's official total exports, which ranged from $20 to $30 billion per year over the decade (Yukseker, 2003).

Although Karov now possessed some capital from the sale of the family property, there was not enough capital to open a store for the luggage traders. More importantly, none of the family members knew how to do business in Turkey. To add to their difficulties, because they had all grown up in Bulgaria, they spoke Bulgarian and Russian very well, but their command of the Turkish language was limited.

Karov considered these obstacles carefully and arrived at a solution that would address each one. After consulting his family, he contacted a friend—a Yugoslavian immigrant in Turkey—who owned a business that manufactured leather wallets under the Jenni brand name. Karov proposed a partnership in which he would open a store in the Laleli district and sell Jenni products to entrepreneurs from Russia and Eastern Europe. Although Jenni had sold leather goods in the Turkish market for almost 30 years, it was not a well-known brand; in fact, in recent years, the financial health of the company had deteriorated sharply. Karov's offer, therefore, suited both parties. It was agreed that Karov would own just ten percent of the store, reflecting the fact that his partner would provide the initial capital to establish the venture.

The store, which opened in November 1991, was an immediate success. The demand for Jenni products among the luggage traders was strong, and the company sold 210,000 items in the first year alone. From the very beginning, the transactions between Karov and the luggage traders were based on mutual trust and a sense of shared experience of living under communism. Karov would even allow some customers to purchase goods on account and bring the money back to him once they had sold them in their home markets.

In the beginning, virtually all of the products bought by the luggage traders were sold in street markets in their home countries. The large department stores in the transition economies were still state owned, and there were not yet any private stores or boutiques. However, even in the street markets, Karov insisted the products be displayed with a sign featuring the brand name, Jenni, and sold in Jenni branded shopping bags.

In 1994, Karov took a risky step and invited 20 of his most-trusted Russian traders to open official Jenni stores in Moscow. This move included a new organizational structure based on the appointment of a main distributor in each city who was responsible for selling Jenni products to the retailers in the city in which they were located.

By conferring ownership and responsibility onto these distributors, Karov believed they would come to see the brand as their own and be more likely to work constructively with him to develop the brand. In addition, Karov sought to convey to his distributors that they were not engaged in a purely commercial relationship. Instead, he emphasized that they were friends and partners who shared a common history and whose interests were intertwined; they were the new entrepreneurs who had emerged from the former communist system and were taking advantage of the opportunities offered by the transition to a market economy.

Establishing a distribution network not only strengthened the Jenni brand by moving the products out of the street markets and into stores, but also allowed Karov access to a very large market whose laws, regulations, and business conventions were very unfamiliar to him. He was able to circumvent many of the difficult issues associated with doing business in Russia by relying on his distributors' knowledge and contacts. This meant that he was also able to avoid dealing with corrupt officials and any involvement in unlawful business dealings.

However, at the same time as the business was rapidly expanding, Karov's relationship with his partner in Turkey (the owner of Jenni) was becoming increasingly fractious. In particular, Karov was unhappy that his partner's sons had taken a substantive stake in the business, while he was unable to bring any of his own family members into the venture.

Karov discussed his discontent with his partner and openly declared that he wanted to create his own leather goods business using the distribution network that he had developed while selling Jenni products from the store in Istanbul. His partner agreed on the condition that Karov would continue to distribute the Jenni brand in the Russian market. He appeared unconcerned that the two brands might be in competition, believing it unlikely that Karov could build a business that would threaten the Jenni brand.

During 1999, Karov entered the Russian market with his own brand, which he named after his daughter, Neroli. He took the opportunity to make his business a family business and quickly involved family members in key positions. His wife soon joined him in the store and took on the crucial role of managing relationships with the firm's distributors. Karov also made his brothers partners in the firm despite the fact that they did not invest any capital. He said it was not acceptable to ask for financial input from his closest family members and that the help and trust they provided was worth more to him than money. Besides, he felt that it was his obligation as the eldest brother to provide for the family.

Karov's generosity, however, did not stop at his closest family members. He also employed his more distant relatives and a significant number of Turkish Bulgarian immigrants, many of whom had struggled to find employment in Turkey. Some of them had already worked for him at the Jenni manufacturing plant but were keen to move to Neroli and to help him with this new endeavor, in part because they felt "obligated towards someone from [our] kin."

From the outset there was strong interest in the new brand from Karov's Russian distributors; indeed, the relationship between Karov and his distributors was critical to the operation of the new business. Consider the following quotation from a Ukrainian distributor:

> This is not about a brand. It is much more about the people. All my transactions with the Jenni brand have always been with Karov and I would not want to work with someone else. If Karov sells X brand, I will have that in my store. If one day, he sells clothes, I will sell that. I trust him. He is a good businessman... a good person.

Within a year, Neroli began to outperform Jenni in terms of sales. There were several reasons for Neroli's strong performance. First, Neroli worked with well-known Italian designers and suppliers, and the products were of much higher quality. Second, the Russian distributors trusted Karov and had worked with him for some time. Third, perhaps most importantly, the Neroli brand proved popular with Russian consumers. By 2005, Karov had established a network of 87 stores in nine countries, with combined sales of almost 700,000 units per year.

However, despite these successes, the reliance on this extended network of family and friendship ties began to inhibit the development of the firm in some important respects. In particular, Karov frequently recounted the problems of finding suitably qualified personnel, especially in professional roles like accounting and marketing. He also struggled to find a reliable English translator (in his own words, he "only" speaks Russian, Bulgarian, and Turkish); this proved to be a major stumbling block in his unsuccessful attempts to expand into Western Europe and North America. Moreover, during the data collection it was striking that almost everyone working in Neroli spoke in the Turkish-Bulgarian dialect rather than Turkish. This made it very hard for any "outsiders" to "fit in." (See Table 2.1 for a summary of the events described in this section.)

Table 2.1 Critical events in the development of Neroli

Approximate dates	Key events and issues	Countries entered
1989–1992	- Karov explores the possibility of selling leather bags and purses to the Russian market. - Karov approaches a Turkish Yugoslavian immigrant who owns a leather factory in Turkey about a possible collaboration.	–
1992–1994	- The two men agree to open a small store in Istanbul (as a joint venture). The store sells a range of leather goods and the products are targeted mainly at Russian tourists. - Karov works hard to build relationships with his Russian retailers and distributors. The business is very profitable, but Karov realizes he must reach more retailers and distributors if he is to realize his ambitions. This leads him to appoint a distributor in a number of Russian cities. He also develops relationships with distributors in Kazakhstan, Byelorussia, Ukraine, and Bulgaria,	Russia, Kazakhstan, Byelorussia, Ukraine, Uzbekistan
1994–1999	- The distribution network in Russia works very well. The network expands to 77 stores across Eastern Europe, Russia, and its former republics, incorporating around 750 people. - In 1999, Karov decides to form his own brand (Neroli) and to source products from a much wider range of manufacturers.	Bulgaria and Azerbaijan
2000–Present	- The network works to expand distribution into the US and the UK but makes little impact - Network members complain that they lack expertise in key areas such as marketing and finance.	Attempting to enter North America and Italy

Learning from Neroli

The case of Neroli provides us with an excellent opportunity to develop a deeper understanding of the effects of family influence on family business. Based on the case analysis, I present three findings. In the first subsection, we will examine the role of altruism in family business and demonstrate how the altruistic behavior exhibited by Karov toward family and near kin was fundamental to the early development of the firm and resulted in reduced agency costs.

In the following subsection, we'll consider how Karov managed to replicate the characteristics of the family, along with the trust and norms of reciprocity that underpin it, to non-family members. This led to the creation of a quasi-family based on distant kinship and ethnic ties and also reduced agency costs as the firm sought to expand.

In the final subsection, we'll examine the limits of altruism in family business. I found that agency costs increased over time as the business developed. Interestingly, however, different kinds of agency costs were evident amongst blood relations and non-blood relations. With respect to family and near kin, agency costs manifested themselves in the form of moral hazard. On the other hand, with respect to quasi-family members connected through distant kinship and ethnic ties, agency costs manifested themselves in the form of adverse selection.

Altruism as a strategy for growth

Altruism, in particular a concern for the welfare of family members and a desire to build a legacy for them, was central to Karov's motivation to build a business and to his approach in managing it. In other words, the existence of Neroli is inextricably intertwined with the altruistic motivations of the founder.

When Karov first founded Neroli, he immediately involved his wife, his brothers, and his sisters-in-law in the new venture. His brothers were given equity in the firm without contributing capital. Crucially, Karov sought to ensure that this involvement was active rather than passive; he worked closely with family members, asking for their input, giving them responsibility for key business functions, and emphasizing their importance to the organization. The sense of belonging and ownership that this engendered appeared to motivate family members to "go the extra mile" for the business.

For example, after having bad experiences with professional drivers who would "come up with all kinds of reasons to rip you off," Karov's brothers offered to take responsibility for transporting Neroli merchandise from Istanbul to destinations around Russia—arduous journeys that involved being away from Istanbul for several weeks at a time. Similarly, Karov's wife and sisters-in-law volunteered to undertake a range of unskilled and unpleasant duties in addition to their existing administrative responsibilities. These involved such tasks as cleaning and packing merchandise in the warehouse to ensure that shipments went out on time.

In addition to Karov's immediate family (i.e., wife, siblings, and children), his kinship network (comprising aunts, uncles, cousins, and friends of the family) also played a key role. This network, like many kinship networks, was characterized by strong ties, a sense of shared cultural identity, and the charisma and leadership capabilities of the central figure (Peng, 2004). In this respect, the Neroli kinship network evokes comparison with Chinese guanxi circles (Wong, 1998); Neroli extended from the center (i.e., Karov), to immediate family members, and then to more distant relatives and family friends.

As Neroli developed, members of the kinship network worked very long hours, often without vacations. Some even slept in the factory to ensure that orders with key distributors were filled during the busiest periods. During the fieldwork, many of them stressed that they were indebted to Karov for offering them employment and were "very well taken care of." In addition, I was told of many acts of generosity by Karov toward his kin. For example, he financed the education of several children of his employees and paid for medical expenses and weddings.

In the early stages of Neroli, the ability to rely on family and near kin afforded the business a high degree of flexibility, and this helped to reduce the risk and uncertainty associated with building a new venture. Karov appeared to have struck the appropriate mix of incentives and managerial control to align the interests of family members. As a result, Neroli benefited from reduced information asymmetries and monitoring costs; this helped to place the business on a solid early footing. These observations are consistent with other findings in family business studies (e.g. Van den Berghe and Carchon, 2003; Zahra, 2005) that suggest that altruistic behavior can reduce agency problems in family firms.

Interestingly, I did not find evidence that Karov used or threatened to use sanctions to discipline family and near kin in the event of malfeasance; nor did he use specific monetary incentives to alter behavior. At this stage in Neroli's development, the altruistic behavior exhibited was reciprocal and symmetrical and appeared to be motivated (on both sides) by a willingness to build and be part of a family institution.

Building the quasi-family

Peredo (2003) introduces the concept of "spiritual kin-based businesses," which she distinguishes from the "blood and marriage kin-based businesses" that dominate the family business literature. In developing this concept, Peredo expands the notion of the family beyond the biological and suggests that groups of individuals use rituals—social, cultural, or religious—in order to "recreate" the characteristics normally attributed to the biological family. Specifically, she suggests that spiritual kin display a series of rights and obligations toward one another. For example, in return for offering support and protection, often in the form of employment, "family" leaders and their organizations are rewarded with high levels of commitment and loyalty.

In seeking to expand Neroli internationally, Karov deliberately attempted to foster this kind of spiritual kin-based business and the sense of obligation and commitment that it implies amongst distant kin and non-family members. Specifically, he used altruism and *shared ethnic identity* as strategic tools in order to create a quasi-family unit. Most significantly, as Karov established his distribution network across the post-Soviet bloc, partners were continually reminded of their "shared experience of communism." Karov actively sought to build links with partners who were immigrants, as this gave him another mechanism through which to leverage a common bond and to build a sense of "family."

In addition to emphasizing common heritage, Karov exhibited extraordinary levels of trust in the early stages of business relationships. For example, he advanced new partners significant levels of stock in the company, often up to $50,000, without any contractual protection in the event of malfeasance. Partners would be invited to repay Karov after the stock had been sold, a highly unusual practice in Turkey and Eastern Europe. This kind of apparently altruistic behavior, combined with an emphasis on shared ethnic identity, fostered very high levels of trust amongst partners. This resulted in a remarkably coherent network that operated ostensibly in the manner of a biological family but extended far beyond its traditional boundaries. Karov referred to his distributors as "friends," while his distributors often referred to him as "family," "father," and "uncle." Consider this quote from an employee at Neroli:

> I will work for Neroli day and night, vacations, weekends…without money even. I trust Karov very much, and I want him to be even more successful. After all, he is an immigrant too, and I would rather help an immigrant like me, than help a local.

Thus, one of Karov's most important strategic assets was his ability to negotiate and renegotiate the boundaries and scope of this quasi-family. This suggests that altruism can be employed by owner-managers to build loyalty and commitment amongst key organizational stakeholders outside of the biological family.

In addition, creating this kind of quasi-family had the effect of aligning the interests of Karov with "family" members: They became "psychologically tied" (Pierce, Kostova, and Dirks, 2001: 299) to the business and responded as if they had a residual claim on the family's estate (Schulze et al., 2003). With respect to the principal-agent relationship, information asymmetries and the costs of monitoring and enforcing agreements were reduced, thereby ameliorating agency problems. While this connection has not explicitly been made in the context of family business studies, organization studies have established the propensity for (non-shareholding) employees to exhibit this kind of psychological ownership in relation to their employing organization (Dirks, Cummings, and Pierce, 1996) and the tasks they perform (Das, 1993).

Note that this conception of ethnicity emphasizes that ethnic identity is socially constructed rather than objectively determined. Indeed, I follow Aldrich and Waldinger (1990: 112) in defining ethnicity as:

> an adjective that refers to differences between categories of people. When "ethnic" is linked to group, it implies that members have some awareness of group membership and a common origin and culture, or that others think of them as having these attributes.
>
> (p. 112)

Moreover, while I acknowledge the significance of Paredo's (2003) contribution (spiritual kin-based businesses), the case of Neroli does not fit neatly with her conception of family. Rather than the simple biological/spiritual dichotomy that Peredo outlined, I observed a more subtle distinction among family, kin, and ethnicity. In this case, the three can perhaps be thought of as a set of concentric circles of decreasing rights and obligations as we move outward from family to kin and finally to ethnicity. I recognize, of course, that the relationship between kinship and ethnicity is not straightforward. Both kinship and ethnicity share the notions of heritage and of distant interconnection. However, while extending kinship through generations involves biological reproduction, extending ethnicity through generations involves social reproduction and the construction of a shared identity.

Therefore, we can conclude that the boundaries of "family" within the family firm are not objective and static, but rather negotiated and fluid. Furthermore, the development of a quasi-family through social connections based on distant kinship and ethnicity (broadly defined) can ameliorate agency costs by aligning the interests of quasi-family members.

The limitations of altruism in family business

As noted, Karov's altruistic behavior toward family, kin, and non-family members linked through ethnic ties created a sense of togetherness and reciprocity that permeated the firm and led to reduced agency costs. However, as the firm grew and became more successful over time, I observed that agency problems became increasingly significant. Interestingly, different agency problems were evident amongst family and near kin and the quasi-family linked through distant kinship and ethnic ties.

With regard to family and near kin, agency problems manifested themselves mainly in the form of moral hazard. Specifically, there was evidence of shirking, free riding, and the overconsumption of perks. For example, Karov's brothers, who played a prominent role in the early days of the venture, became marginal figures with less and less interest in the welfare of the business despite the fact that they had been given equity without investing any capital. According to one respondent: "They [the brothers] like to sit around all day, drinking coffee or playing computer games, while Karov runs this entire business."

It became clear from the interviews that Karov was concerned about the behavior of several family members. Furthermore, his concerns were widely recognized within the firm. As one respondent told me, he "feels helpless, as though his hands have been tied." This kind of behavior posed two problems for Karov. First, it conflicted with his vision of the family working and succeeding together. Second, it created a sense of chronic organizational injustice; some members of the family grew increasingly resentful of what they perceived as equal rewards for unequal effort.

Even so, Karov was unwilling to punish or sanction family and near kin connected with the business; he appeared especially concerned about the ramifications for familial relationships if he were to discipline family members. In other words, Karov prioritized the welfare of the family over and above the welfare of the business. In this way, the behavior of family members was, on one level, rewarded or at least encouraged by the incentive structure that Karov had put in place. As this became increasingly apparent to other family members, the extent to which they shirked and consumed perks increased; they appeared to develop a sense of entitlement in terms of their claim on the business.

With respect to non-blood relations in the quasi-family, on the other hand, increased agency costs manifested themselves primarily in the form of adverse selection. Most obviously, Karov's preference for working with partners that shared the same ethnic heritage and identity severely limited his choice of potential partners. On several occasions, Karov was left exposed as key individuals lacked the skills and competencies to perform specific tasks effectively.

In particular, this selection bias resulted in the firm not having access to skilled professionals in accounting, marketing, and information technology. For example, Karov hired the daughter of a family friend as Neroli's brand manager even though she didn't have any marketing training or related experience. Karov thought that she would quickly learn the necessary skills because her parents had worked in the fashion industry for many years. Over time, however, the limitations of this strategy became increasingly apparent.

Adverse selection was also evident when Neroli sought to expand into markets beyond Eastern Europe. This was dramatically illustrated by Neroli's failed attempt to enter the US market early in 2004. At that time, Karov met Anton (a US-based businessman who had emigrated from Bulgaria to the US in 1991) at a trade fair in Russia. The two men quickly developed a strong relationship, and, despite the fact that Anton knew little about the leather goods industry, Karov was confident that he had found a partner who could fulfill his dream of breaking into the American market. Their relationship was based in part on their shared identity; Karov drew comparisons between his own struggle as an immigrant entrepreneur in Turkey and Anton's ambition to build a life for himself and his family in the US. Karov declared that, "Anton is an immigrant and knows what it is to have the burning desire to earn money."

However, Anton's inexperience in distribution in the fashion industry became obvious very quickly. He was able to sell only a small fraction of the $50,000 of stock that Karov had advanced to him. As of this writing, Neroli has made virtually no impact in the US or Western Europe despite several attempts to do so. While adverse selection is not the only reason for this lack of success, it was clearly an important factor.

My observations about the diverging interests of family members and the problems of monitoring and enforcing contracts are consistent with the recent empirical work of Schulze et al. (2003) and Lubatkin et al. (2005). However, I believe that this study makes an important contribution by making the connection between the temporal maturity of family firms and the likelihood of increased agency costs.

Moreover, by suggesting that different kinds of agency problems apply to different types of "family" members, I begin to develop a "thicker" account of the principal-agent relationship in family firms than has been presented in much of the literature to date.

Conclusions and implications

I began by highlighting the assertion of Chrisman et al. (2005) that a key task for family business researchers is to identify the major differences between family and non-family firms and to ascertain whether these differences have their roots in family involvement. In my study, in common with other scholars in family business studies (e.g. Lubatkin et al., 2005), I argued that altruism is a key distinguishing feature of family business, one with profound implications for the principal-agent relationship. In addition, following Schulze et al. (2003: 488), I suggest that "the economic literature on altruism is a potentially useful resource that promises to... lead researchers towards a richer theory of the family firm."

I believe that this study has made three important contributions to the family business literature, and in particular to developing an understanding of the complex role that altruism plays in family firms. Significantly, the findings enable the apparently conflicting empirical evidence on agency costs and family business to be incorporated into an overarching framework that allows for the possibility that family influence may lead to increased *and* decreased agency problems.

The first contribution is to show that altruism has the potential to align the interests of family members and reduce agency costs in the family firm, *providing it is reciprocal and symmetrical*. This is consistent with the founding fathers of agency theory such as Fama and Jensen (1983) and Jensen and Meckling (1973), as well as some family business researchers (e.g., Eaton et al., 2002) who argued that family ownership is a highly efficient form of organization because information asymmetries and monitoring costs are reduced.

The second contribution is to show that the logic of the family, and altruistic behavior in particular, can be transferred beyond family and near kin in order to build a quasi-family based on distant kinship and ethnic ties. In this respect, there are clear parallels with Paredo's (2003: 398) concept of spiritual kin-based business: "relations marked by social, cultural and religious rituals of incorporation... [through which] the concept of family expands beyond the biological family." Unlike Paredo, however, who suggests that spiritual kin-based business comprises a distinct category of relations that operate separately from the biological family, I conceive of the quasi-family as a set of relations that overlap and are intertwined with the biological family. The study observed a family business in which the owner-manager exhibited a similar set of altruistic behaviors toward blood relations and non-blood relations and was "rewarded" with a reciprocal set of altruistic behaviors in return. This further reduced problems of agency and was crucial to Neroli's successful attempts to expand into new markets.

The third contribution is to show that there are limits to altruism as family businesses become larger and more mature. Specifically, and broadly consistent with Gomez-Mejia et al. (2001) and Schulze et al. (2003), the study demonstrated that altruism became unbalanced and agency costs increased. Interestingly, the agency problems were different with respect to family members and near kin on the one hand and quasi-family members and distant kin on the other. Family members were observed to engage in moral hazard, in particular to shirk, free ride, and consume excessive perks. While Karov was very concerned about this behavior, he did not seek to sanction family and near kin, nor did he offer financial incentives to alter their behavior, a practice that has been shown to reduce moral hazard in other family firms (Schulze et al., 2003).

The dominant agency cost with respect to quasi-family members was adverse selection. Specifically, the firm struggled to find suitably qualified professionals. Neroli also had problems finding effective distribution partners outside of Eastern Europe, in places where it was more difficult to find partners linked through ethnic ties. This was a significant factor behind Neroli's failed attempts to expand into Western Europe and North America.

Caveats and limitations

Taken together, I believe that the findings represent an important step forward in developing a more complete theory of the family firm as well as augmenting existing insights about the effects of altruism on agency costs in family business. However, given that the findings are based on a single case study and that the geographical and socio-political context of the case is quite unique, one must be cautious about generalizing from the research.

Nevertheless, it is my view that the findings about altruism and agency costs have the potential to be generalized to family businesses in other contexts, including Western Europe and North America; after all, family-based altruism is a universal concept, and I believe that it is likely to manifest itself in similar ways in family businesses across cultures. However, the findings about the role of the quasi-family in family business might be less generalizable. Although owner-managers of family firms are likely to exhibit altruistic behavior toward non-family members in different settings, the ways that different ethnic groups relate to one another and respond to altruistic behavior are likely to differ.

Directions for future research

This study suggests a number of directions for future research. Most obviously, given that it relies upon a single case study, further research involving large samples of family firms in different settings is needed in order to test the robustness of the findings. Of particular interest is the extent to which the changing pattern of agency costs holds across family businesses in different jurisdictions. Do agency costs tend to be correlated to firm size and age? What other factors are likely to influence the evolution of the principal-agent relationship in family firms?

A second direction for future research concerns the role of the quasi-family in different settings. I have conceptualized ethnicity as being socially constructed. In the case study, it was based around a shared experience of living under communism. I suggest that an interesting question is the extent to which the nature of the bond that binds particular ethnic groups effects the formation of the quasi-family. For example, if ethnicity were based around university ties or religious affiliation, would the dynamics of the quasi-family differ?

Finally, this study raises important questions about the propensity of family firms to engage in international business. There are relatively few studies that examine this issue, and even fewer that consider new ventures that internationalize from inception. Of particular interest are the effects of family influence on the propensity and capacity of family firms to internationalize. Given the findings, it seems possible that the family and quasi-family provide an effective route to internationalization. However, it's clear that we need further research to more fully understand the role of family influence in the internationalization process of family firms.

Notes

1 The names of companies and individuals have been disguised to protect confidentiality.
2 There is, however, disagreement about the range of non-economic goals that family businesses pursue (Sharma, Chrisman and Chua, 1997).

3 Cited in Chrisman et al. (2005).
4 While this personal knowledge was advantageous in terms of access and understanding the dynamics of the firm, there are obvious dangers in terms of objectivity. The authors sought to address this point by reflecting back the findings to key respondents on several occasions. Moreover, although the data were collected mostly by one person, there were three researchers involved in data analysis and writing up the project. All of the researchers met with the focal entrepreneur and talked with him at length about the case and our interpretation of the salient issues.

References

Alchian, A. & Woodward, S. (1988). The firm is dead; long live the firm: A review of Oliver Williamson's the economic institutions of capitalism. *Journal of Economic Literature*, 26, 65–79.

Aldrich, H.E. & Waldinger, R. (1990). Ethnicity and entrepreneurship. *Annual Review of Sociology*, 16, 111–135.

Bijker, W.B., Hughes, T.P., & Pinch, T. (1987). *The social construction of technological systems*. Cambridge, MA: MIT Press.

Bjornberg, A., Elstrodt, H.-P., & Pandit, V. (2014). The family-business factor in emerging markets. *McKinsey Quarterly*, December, pp. 1–6.

Carney, M. (2005). Corporate governance and competitive advantage in family-controlled firms. *Entrepreneurship Theory and Practice*, 29, 249–265.

Chami, R. (1997). *What's different about family business? Social science research network: Organizations and market abstracts*. Working Paper Series, file no. 98061505.

Chrisman, J.J., Chua, J.H., & Litz, R. (2004). Comparing the agency costs of family and non-family firms: Conceptual issues and exploratory evidence. *Entrepreneurship Theory and Practice*, 28(4), 335–354.

Chrisman, J.J., Chua, J.H., & Sharma, P. (2005). Trends and directions in the development of a strategic management theory of the family firm. *Entrepreneurship Theory and Practice*, 29(5), 555–575.

Chua, J.J. & Schnabel, J. (1986). Nonpecuniary benefits and asset market equilibrium. *Financial Review*, 21(2), 112–118.

Daily, C.M. & Dollinger, M.J. (1992). An empirical examination of ownership structure in family and professionally managed firms. *Family Business Review*, 4(2), 117–135.

Das, G. (1993). Local memoirs of a global manager. *Harvard Business Review*, 71(2), 38–47.

Dirks, K.T., Cummings, L.L., & Pearce, J.L. (1996). Psychological ownership in organizations: Conditions under which individuals promote and resist change. In R.W. Woodman & W.A. Pasmore (eds.), *Research in organizational change and development*, vol. 9, 1–23. Greenwich, CT: JAI Press.

Dyer, Jr., W.G. (2003). The family: The missing variable in organizational research. *Entrepreneurship Theory and Practice*, 27(4), 401–416.

Eaton, C., Yuan, L., & Wu, Z. (2002). *Reciprocal altruism and the theory of the family firm*. Paper presented at the Second Annual Conference on

Theories of the Family Enterprise: Search for a Paradigm, Wharton School of Business, Philadelphia, December.

Eisenhardt, K.M. (1989a). Agency theory: An assessment and review. *Academy of Management Review*, 14(1), 57–74.

Eisenhardt, K.M. (1989b). Building theories from case study research. *Academy of Management Review*, 14, 532–550.

Fama, E.F. & Jensen, M.C. (1983). Separation of ownership and control. *Journal of Law and Economics*, 26(2), 301–325.

Fama, E.F. & Jensen, M.C. (1985). Organizational forms and investment decisions. *Journal of Financial Economics*, 14, 101–109.

Garud, R. & Rappa, M.A. (1994). A Socio-cognitive model of technological evolution: The case of cochlear implants. *Organization Science*, 5(3), 344–362.

Garud, R., Sanjay J., & Arun K., (2002). Institutional entrepreneurship in the sponsorship of common technological standards: The case of Sun Microsystems and Java. *Academy of Management Journal*, 45, 196–214.

Gomez-Meija, Luis R., Nunez-Nickel, M., & Gutierrez, I. (2001). The role of family ties in agency contracts. *Academy of Management Journal*, 44(1), 81–95.

Jensen, M.C. & Meckling, W.F. (1976). Theory of the firm: Managerial behaviour, agency costs and ownership structure. *Journal of Financial Economics*, 3, 305–360.

Kang, D. (2000). The impact of family ownership on performance in public organizations: A study of the U.S. Fortune 500, 1982–1994. *2000 Academy of Management Meetings*, Toronto, Canada.

Karra, N. (2005). An analysis of Factors Explaining Accelerated Internationalization Process in Born-Global Firms. Ph.D. Dissertation, University of Cambridge.

Lubatkin, M.H., Schulze, W.S., Ling, Y., & Dino, R. (2005). The effects of parental altruism on the governance of family-managed firms. *Journal of Organizational Behavior*, 26, 313–330.

Peng, Y. (2004). Kinship networks and entrepreneurs in China's transitional economy. *American Journal of Sociology*, 109(5), 1045–1075.

Peredo, A.M. (2003). Nothing thicker than blood: Commentary on "Help one another, use one another: Toward an anthropology of family business." *Entrepreneurship Theory and Practice*, 27(4), 383–396.

Pierce, J.L., Kostova, T., & Dirks, K.T. (2001). Toward a theory of psychological ownership in organizations. *Academy of Management Review*, 26(2), 298–310.

Schulze, W.S., Lubatkin, M.H., & Dino, R.N. (2003). Toward a theory of agency and altruism in family firms. *Journal of Business Venturing*, 18(4), 473–491.

Sharma, P., Chrisman, J.J., & Chua, J.H. (1997). Strategic management of the family business: Past research and future challenges. *Family Business Review*, 10, 1–35.

Van den Berghe, L.A.A. & Carchon, S. (2003). Agency relations within the family business system: An exploratory approach. *Corporate Governance: An International Review*, 11(3), 171–180.

Wong, Y.H. (1998). The dynamic of guanxi in China. *Singapore Management Review*, 20(2), 25.

Yin, R.K. (1994). *Case study research: Design and methods, third edition*. Thousand Oaks, CA: Sage Publications.

Yukseker, D. (2003). *Laleli-MoskovaMekiği: Kayıtdışı Ticaret ve Cinsiyet İlişkileri* [The Laleli-Moscow Shuttle: Informal Trade and Gender Relations]. İstanbul: İletişim Yayınları.

Zahra, S. (2003). International expansion of US manufacturing family businesses: The effect of ownership and involvement. *Journal of Business Venturing*, 18(4), 495–512.

Zahra, S. (2005). Entrepreneurial risk taking in family firms. *Family Business Review*, 18(1), 23–40.

3   Building a business on ethnic ties

A study of the effects of ethnic networks on entrepreneurial activities

The literature on entrepreneurship has paid considerable attention to the role of ethnicity in new venture formation. However, there has been comparatively little attention paid to the role of ethnic ties in new ventures *after* founding. In this chapter, we will continue to discuss the results of a case study of an international network of high-end fashion leather goods producers, distributors, and retailers in Russia, Eastern Europe, and the Middle East.

This study leads us to the conclusion that while ethnic ties can be an important resource when founding a new venture, these same ethnic ties can become increasingly limiting as constituent firms grow and develop. The study demonstrates how ethnic ties can both enable and constrain, and it explains how and why their dynamics change over time.

The important role of ethnicity in facilitating entrepreneurship has been widely recognized in the entrepreneurship literature (e.g., Light, 1972; Waldinger, 1986; Butler and Greene, 1997; Greve and Salaff, 2003). Aldrich and Waldinger (1990: 113), for example, begin their work on the subject with the observation that "some ethnic groups, particularly among first and second generation immigrants, have higher rates of business formation and ownership than do others." The question of why some immigrant groups are more likely to found new ventures than others, and in some cases more likely than the broader majority population, has important ramifications for entrepreneurship research, practice, and policy (Barrett, Jones, and McEvoy, 1996; Light and Gold, 2000). This question has led to much theorizing in the area (e.g., Bonacich, 1973; Wilson and Portes, 1980; Mars and Ward, 1984; Waldinger, 1986; Light and Bonacich, 1988; Portes and Jensen, 1989, Dijst and van Kempen, 1991).

At the same time, this narrow emphasis on how and why members of various ethnic groups *create* new businesses has resulted in the neglect of "other aspects of business activity such as management and growth"

(Dyer and Ross, 2000: 48). In this chapter, we will begin to redress this imbalance by examining how ethnic networks facilitate on-going management and growth *after* founding. This study goes beyond the examination of the start-up phase and looks at the effects of the network dynamics of ethnic entrepreneurship from inception to relative maturity. In other words, we will begin to heed Dyer and Ross (2000: 48) and work to develop "a better understanding of the social networks within which entrepreneurs continue to develop their operations."

More specifically, the study presented in this chapter adds to our understanding of the link between ethnic networks and entrepreneurship through an in-depth case study of ethnic entrepreneurs. These entrepreneurs are part of a highly successful, international network of high-end fashion leather goods producers, distributors, and retailers in Russia, Eastern Europe, and the Middle East. The network is composed mainly of Balkan immigrants who left their respective countries and settled abroad. Their selective migration and settlement resulted in the emergence of trading networks or trading diasporas (Sowell, 1996) that "pursue different strategies than the majority" (Iyer and Shapiro, 1999: 84).

This study makes several contributions to the literature on ethnic entrepreneurship. First, it presents a model of the role of ethnic networks in new venture formation and growth. The model builds on the existing literature but adds an important time dimension. We will see how the same ties that enable during the formation and early growth phase come to limit and constrain as the new venture grows and develops. Second, we will observe exactly how these ties enable and constrain and view an initial classification of the enabling and constraining forces. Third, instead of looking at entrepreneurs as individuals, the study examines an entire network with the intent of developing an understanding of the complex network dynamics that characterize ethnic entrepreneurship. Fourth, the research focuses on a sophisticated, highly successful international network that has grown very rapidly since its founding less than 10 years ago. Case study researchers often recommend extreme or polar cases because the constructs of interest tend to be more "transparent and observable" to the researcher (Eisenhardt, 1989). In this case, the network dynamics that have driven growth, as well as the difficulties of managing them, are highlighted by the rapid expansion and success of the network. Fifth, I have focused on a network of ethnic entrepreneurs in a very different geographic location from that addressed in the existing literature. Where most of the studies to date have focused on ethnic enclaves in developed economies in the West, this study targets a broad ethnic community spanning transition and developing economies in Russia, the former Eastern Bloc, and Turkey.

This section will proceed in four steps. I'll begin with a review of the ethnic entrepreneurship literature and present the research question. Next, I'll discuss the methodology and introduce the empirical context of the study. Third, we'll look at a model of the factors that influence the success or failure of such ventures and how these factors vary over time. And we'll conclude with a discussion of the complex relationship between ethnicity and entrepreneurship and suggest some directions for further research.

Ethnicity and ethnic entrepreneurship

Ethnic entrepreneurship can be broadly defined as business ownership by immigrant and ethnic-group members (Light and Bonacich, 1988; Waldinger, 1986; Waldinger et al., 1990). In an early work on the subject, Simmel (1950) focuses on "traders" as "strangers" and the effect that their status as outsiders has on their business dealings. More recently, Chaganti and Greene (2002: 128) define the related term "minority entrepreneur" as any business owner "who is not of the majority population." Similarly, Butler and Greene (1997) define "immigrant entrepreneur" as an "individual who as a recent arrival in the country starts a business as a means of survival." In all these cases, there is an attempt to differentiate between a majority population and some distinguishable minority population.

This paper follows Aldrich and Waldinger (1990: 112) in defining "ethnic" as:

> an adjective that refers to differences between categories of people. When "ethnic" is linked to group, it implies that members have some awareness of group membership and a common origin and culture, or that others think of them as having these attributes.

Waldinger, Aldrich, and Ward (1990: 3) build on this understanding of ethnic to define ethnic entrepreneurship as entrepreneurship characterized by "a set of connections and regular patterns of interaction among people sharing common national background or migration experience." This definition forms the basis of the work here, but I need to add one more element to their definition of "ethnic." I define ethnic entrepreneurship as

> entrepreneurship characterized by a set of connections and regular patterns of interaction among a group of people with a mutual

awareness of group membership based on patterns of migration, common origin, or other cultural characteristics that separate them from the majority population.

Light's (1972) *Ethnic Enterprise in America* is the first major contribution to our understanding of the dynamics of ethnic entrepreneurship. This study led to the emergence of a stream of literature on ethnic entrepreneurship more or less as it is defined above. The two most prominent early models are the "middleman minorities" (Bonacich, 1973) and "ethnic enclaves" perspectives (Wilson and Martin, 1982; Portes, 1989).

The middleman minorities approach suggests that firms use ethnic entrepreneurs as negotiators to attract cheap labor in order to reduce their production costs (Bonacich, 1973). Unlike enclave theory, middleman minority theory is not concerned with where enterprises are located but with the role they play in facilitating markets. As the term suggests, these studies concentrate on how ethnic groups act as middlemen in the movement of goods and services. Historically, members of these groups have tended to be self-employed and to engage in activities such as labor contracting, lending, brokering, and rent collecting. As middlemen, these entrepreneurs negotiate arrangements between producers and consumers, owners and renters, elites and masses, and employers and employees (Bonacich and Modell, 1980). These businesses are found primarily in the retail and service sectors.

The literature on ethnic enclaves, on the other hand, focuses on "immigrant groups who concentrate in a specific location and organize a variety of enterprises serving their own ethnic market and/or the general population" (Portes, 1981: 290–291). These enclaves are characterized by co-location and co-ethnicity (Portes, 1981). This body of work suggests that ethnic entrepreneurs accumulate social capital from their social networks and are more likely and better placed to take advantage of the business networks in the enclave than outsiders. In a similar vein, Light (1984) suggests that ethnic groups are likely to obtain a high degree of unity and social cohesion due to their marginalized status. These entrepreneurs and their co-ethnic employees are also likely to benefit from the resources afforded by proximity and high levels of social cohesion (Iyer and Shapiro, 1999).

While these contributions represent important steps in understanding ethnic entrepreneurship, they have also been criticized for their relatively narrow scope. There have been calls for the development of more sophisticated and wide-ranging theoretical approaches (e.g., Marger and Hoffman, 1992). Aldrich and Waldinger's (1990) framework can be seen as the first and most comprehensive attempt in this respect.

These authors emphasize the often-disadvantaged position of ethnic groups in the countries to which they have emigrated and suggest that initial business opportunities are more likely to be found within ethnic markets. They also point out that further business growth is possible if ethnic businesses cater to non-ethnic communities as well (Aldrich and Waldinger, 1990; Lerner and Khavul, 2003). They add that ethnic forays into non-ethnic markets are usually focused in those niches that (a) are underserved or abandoned by the large mass-marketing organizations, (b) require low economies of scale, (c) have low or unstable market demand, and (d) are characterized by exotic demand. Building on this line of argument, Iyer and Shapiro (1999) stress that some market and industry conditions that are difficult, risky, or simply undoable for large businesses may seem viable and even attractive to ethnic businesses. However, they too speculate that harsh business and economic conditions in their country of origin may be the most significant reason ethnic groups are much more likely to engage in such activities.

A feature of this work is its emphasis on the challenges faced by ethnic minorities: racial hostility, prejudice, discrimination, and disadvantages in the labor market such as a lack of language skills and recognized qualifications. Faced with such conditions, members of ethnic groups are forced to turn to their family and community networks for employment and business opportunities (Light, 1972; Iyer and Shapiro, 1999). However, as Portes (1989: 930) points out, there has been a gradual change toward a more positive characterization of ethnic enterprise as a means for economic advancement (Light, 1984; Waldinger, 1986). Research on ethnic groups has begun to move away from a focus on the hardships they face to the circumstances that may lead them to create alternative social and economic outcomes.

Most notably, Iyer and Shapiro (1999) propose an evolutionary ethnic entrepreneurial business model that is quite different from previous theories and arguments. Their framework considers ethnic groups not only as small businesses operating in niches and catering to the needs of ethnic clientele, but also as international enterprises. They argue that ethnic entrepreneurs tend to begin by supplying co-ethnic labor in an ethnic enclave. Initial business ventures tend to focus on serving local markets within the enclave. Eventually, these ethnic entrepreneurs might expand horizontally into non-ethnic markets and/ or start to invest back in their homelands. They may even expand the business internationally by leveraging their ties in their countries of origin. The outcome is often a set of lateral connections among multiple business interests in their countries of origin and in their new countries. For example, the offshore Chinese population has been very successful at creating these sorts of business networks. However, while this line of argument is an attempt to show that international new ventures can be built on ethnic ties, it assumes that such international expansion will only be possible because of the ethnic and friendship ties in the entrepreneur's country of origin. The existing literature does not yet include an examination of a set of firms that successfully build international new ventures by relying on their ethnic ties to countries other than their country of origin.

In addition, at the core of the ethnic entrepreneurship literature is the assumption that ethnic groups are vulnerable, with limited opportunities and resources, and that the ambition to found a business venture stems from a lack of alternatives. In some instances, ethnic entrepreneurial ventures are assumed to be only small enterprises that "tend to occupy mainly traditional business lines dominated by small firms, and only seldom do they grow into larger firms and shift to more advanced and profitable business fields" (Lerner and Khavul, 2003: 6).

I believe that the focus in the existing literature on these small, specialized enterprises, and on why and how they are founded, is useful but somewhat limited. While many firms founded by ethnic entrepreneurs are small and focus on ethnic enclaves and specialized niches, even casual observation suggests that many are not. Certain questions need to be answered. First, what role do ethnic networks have in the founding and growth of the firms that do not fit this description? Second, how well does the existing literature explain the dynamics of ethnic entrepreneurship that occur around these firms as they grow and develop? This study begins to answer these questions by focusing on a network that is not oriented toward an ethnic enclave—nor is it the sort of firm discussed in the middleman minority literature. However, this network was founded by an ethnic entrepreneur who built upon his ethnic ties. It is therefore a very useful research site for exploring the broader applicability of the existing models of ethnic entrepreneurship and extending the discussion to these important alternative forms.

Methodology

In this section, I'll discuss the research site and explain how I proceeded with data collection and analysis. It is worth noting that my choice of case study was based on both theoretical and practical considerations. From a theoretical point of view, case studies are particularly useful for theory building (Yin, 2003). Given the relative scarcity of empirical work in this area, case study research is arguably the most appropriate approach for extending our understanding of ethnic entrepreneurship. From a practical point of view, there is very little reliable and publicly available data on the topic, particularly outside of North America and Western Europe, making broad demographic studies very difficult. In any case, the existing literature highlights the limitations of understanding ethnic entrepreneurship in terms of size, prevalence, and key characteristics or traits (Iyer and Shapiro, 1999; Aldrich and Waldinger, 1990). Furthermore, while survey-based research was an option, based on my experience, I believed that ethnic entrepreneurs are even less likely to accurately disclose detailed information about their businesses than are traditional entrepreneurs—with whom this problem has been widely encountered. Faced with these challenges in investigating ethnic entrepreneurs and their networks, researchers tend to use case studies to gain deeper insight (Aldrich and Waldinger, 1990). This is the method that I chose as well.

The research site: an international entrepreneurial network

The network of ethnic entrepreneurs that I studied was established by Ishmael Karov, the owner of Neroli. Neroli is a highly successful fashion firm based in Istanbul, Turkey. In the fieldwork I investigated all of the important ethnic ties that had developed around this one focal firm. The network is shown diagrammatically in Figure 3.1.

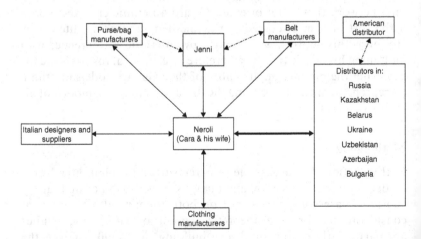

Figure 3.1 The Neroli network.

I selected this case study for several reasons. First, the selection has "rare or unique" qualities that made it a logical candidate for "theoretical sampling" (Eisenhardt, 1989; Yin, 2003). Preliminary research revealed that it was a particularly good example of a highly internationalized ethnic network. The central firm, Neroli, had never had any substantial portion of sales in its domestic market, and, although it was founded in Turkey, it had always exported its entire production through the network. In addition, the size and the type of the network were very different from those in other studies as it encompassed members from Turkey, Eastern Europe, and the former Soviet Union. Finally, the network was highly successful, having grown dramatically in its 10 years of existence. These three factors distinguish this case from more traditional research into ethnic entrepreneurship and therefore, I believe, increase the potential contribution of the case study.

Second, because the focal firm and network were only a decade old, almost all the key members still owned their own companies or stores. This insured that the details of the founding of the central firm and the early development of the network were still fresh in the minds of the interviewees and that the motivations and direct experience of the members were readily available.

Finally, because I had worked for several years for the focal firm as a translator, the network participants were very cooperative and happy to work with me. While working as a translator, I attended many important meetings, was very familiar with the early phase development of the network, and knew many of the ethnic entrepreneurs who were network members. I, therefore, had extensive access to the organization, and the members provided me with any information I requested. I was also able to return to the main firm, Neroli, on multiple occasions to gather further data and to reflect back on my understandings of the case.

Data collection

The primary data source consisted of semi-structured interviews with members of the network, related companies, clients, and suppliers. In total, 66 interviews were conducted with 26 respondents. Several of the respondents were interviewed on multiple occasions. A list of the interviewees is given in Table 3.1.

I began the study by interviewing the owners of Neroli and several of its key employees. During these initial interviews, I asked for names of other entrepreneurs in their network who were then contacted and interviewed. All of these entrepreneurs consented to participate in the study. The advantage of using this technique was that it allowed relatively easy access to other members of the network through those

Table 3.1 List of respondents

Respondents	Geographic location	Type	# of times interviewed	# of times observed at a meeting
Ishmael Karov	Istanbul, Moscow, and Italy	Face to face, telephone, email, fax	7	8
Wife	Istanbul	face to face, telephone	3	
Translators (Neroli)	Istanbul and Moscow	Telephone and face to face	2	5
Employees (Neroli)	Istanbul	Face to face	5	
Employees (Neroli)	Moscow	Face to face	7	
Kamal, owner of Jenni	Istanbul	Face to face	1	1
Belt manufacturer	Istanbul	Face to face	1	1
Bag manufacturer	Istanbul	Face to face	2	1
Leather supplier 1	Istanbul	Face to face	1	
Leather supplier 2	Istanbul	Face to face	1	
Distributor 1	Moscow	Face to face, telephone	3	1
Retailer 1	Moscow	Face to face	1	1
Retailer 2	Kiev, Ukraine	Telephone	2	
Distributor 2	Baku, Azerbaijan	Face to face	1	1
Distributor 3	Kazakhstan	Face to face	1	
Retailer 3	Chelyabinsk, Russia	Telephone	2	
Entrepreneur 1 (luggage trade area)	Istanbul	Face to face	1	
Entrepreneur 2	Istanbul and Moscow	Face to face	2	
Marketing manager of Neroli	Moscow	Face to face	3	1
Italian supplier 1	Firenze	Face to face	2	1
Italian supplier 2	Bologna	Telephone, email and face to face	4	1
Italian designer	Firenze and Bologna	Telephone, face to face, Email	3	1
Italian supplier 3	Milano	Face to face	2	
Men's clothing producer	Eskishehir, Turkey	Telephone	2	1
Store manager 1 (men's clothing line)	Moscow, Russia Sofia, Bulgaria	Face to face, telephone, emails	5	
Total			66 interviews	24

already interviewed, and it ensured that I followed the most significant links in the network. It is very unlikely that they would have been willing to disclose information about their business ventures without the introductions from the founder of the focal firm. By employing this technique, I found respondents to be very cooperative, and I was able to secure access to everyone identified as key members in the network.

I conducted interviews and collected archival data during several trips to Turkey, Russia, Kazakhstan, Azerbaijan, Bulgaria, and Italy. This phase of the data collection was greatly facilitated by attending and observing business meetings where many members of the network were present from disparate geographic locations. In addition, I conducted a number of telephone interviews with network members in Chelyabinsk (Russia), Kiev (Ukraine), Bologna and Milan (Italy), and Sofia (Bulgaria). I speak Turkish, Russian, and Bulgarian and have a working knowledge of Italian, so the interviews were carried out in the language of choice of the interviewee. I also collected substantial secondary data in order to understand the economic and political context within which the firm was founded.

Data analysis

The data was analyzed in three main stages. In the first, the case study data were organized into an "event history database" (Garud and Rappa, 1994; Van de Ven and Poole, 1990). This was done by chronologically ordering descriptions of events taken from the raw data—interview transcripts, field notes, and secondary sources such as journalists' accounts of the political and economic context—and juxtaposing multiple accounts against each other to ascertain the degree of convergence. From this, I developed a narrative of the formation and development of the ethnic network focusing particularly on the role of ethnic ties.

In the second stage, the interview transcripts were coded and notes for references to the primary concepts identified in the research questions. Coding proceeded, initially, on two levels: (1) using a lexicon of concrete terms grounded in the data (e.g., "motivations," "trust," "risk," etc.) and (2) using a lexicon of more abstract terms arising from "the *a priori* specification of constructs" (Eisenhardt, 1989). These terms, like "shared history," "common background," "cultural knowledge," etc., can be found in the literatures on ethnic entrepreneurship. The analysis continued iteratively, moving among data, emerging patterns, and existing theory and research until the patterns were refined into adequate conceptual categories (Eisenhardt, 1989).

A third and final stage of "enfolding findings with the literature" (Eisenhardt, 1989) brought together, iteratively, findings from the previous stages and related them to the literature on ethnic entrepreneurship. I worked back and forth among the raw data, the narrative I had developed regarding the founding and development of the network, and the literature in order to develop a model of the role and dynamics of ethnic ties in the development of the network. This permitted me to synthesize and anchor the findings in a theoretical manner.

NEROLI: a case of successful ethnic entrepreneurship

In this section, I will present the historical background to the case study and introduce the case itself. Some understanding of the complex historical context of the study is necessary in order to show the important role of ethnicity in the development and success of the network of entrepreneurs that surrounds Neroli. We will begin by discussing the historical background of the firm in greater detail than the brief outline in Chapter 1.

Historical background

There are two main events that set the stage for the development of the complex ethnic networks upon which Neroli was founded. First, between June and August 1989, more than 360,000 Bulgarians of Turkish ethnicity currently living in Bulgaria were forced to emigrate to Turkey. The resulting exodus was described as "the largest collective civilian migration since the Second World War" by international humanitarian relief organizations. Here's a description:

> Lines of trucks, cars, and buses could be seen throughout the region, each piled high with people and whatever belongings they had been able to grab hold of and fit into the vehicles in a short time. Those who left abandoned home, land, and whatever they were unable to carry. In some cases, elderly and very young family members were also left behind.
>
> (Pickles, 2001: 1)

This eviction/emigration, ironically called "The Great Excursion," was the final chapter in an intense assimilation process carried out by the Zhivkov government from 1984 to 1989 against ethnic minorities, particularly Turkish Bulgarians. The goal was the creation of a modern Bulgarian nation of pure Slavic citizens. Those who left Bulgaria settled either in immigrant camps set up by the Turkish government or moved into relatives' homes, usually in informal ethnic communities that had been established years before during other "excursions" from Bulgaria, in 1954, 1968, and 1978.

The second important historical event that frames the study took place in 1989 with the fall of the Berlin Wall. This event set off the transition of Soviet bloc countries from centrally planned economies to market economies with multiparty legislative democracies. The effects of this transition were dramatic, not least in terms of the everyday lives of the general public; among other things, it created a rapid expansion of consumer options and entrepreneurial opportunities.

After the transition, numerous entrepreneurial start-ups appeared throughout the former Communist bloc. While these were extremely varied, perhaps the most common form of entrepreneurship was citizens from the post-Soviet bloc and Eastern Europe traveling to neighboring countries, purchasing goods, and bringing them back for sale in their countries. These "luggage traders" were responding to the great demand for Western-style goods in their newly liberated economies.

For Turkey, the luggage traders were an unexpected, but very welcome, export opportunity. At the time, Russian, Bulgarian, and Romanian traders, in particular, came to Istanbul's Laleli and Beyazit districts to purchase clothes, leather goods, and bags, which they then took back to their home markets. This trade, although largely unofficial, reached an estimated US$8.8 billion by 1998, significantly higher than Turkey's official figure, which ranged from $20 to $30 billion per year over the decade.[1] These events provided opportunities for many Turkish businessmen, as well as for many post-socialist entrepreneurs.

Neroli: an ethnic entrepreneurial network

As we discussed above, this study focused on an entrepreneurial network created by Ishmael Karov around a focal firm (Neroli) that produced high-quality leather goods in Turkey for export to Russia and Eastern Europe. Karov was one of the entrepreneurs who benefited from the opportunities arising from the luggage trade. He was also one of the 360,000 Turkish Bulgarians who left their homeland behind to make a new beginning in Istanbul, Turkey, in June of 1989. As a Turkish Bulgarian, he was in an ideal position to build on his knowledge of the Turkish language and culture and his knowledge of Russia and the former Soviet Union to forge an ethnic network to support his new venture. In this section, we'll observe the development of the network in four stages. Due to the constraints of space, and the complexity of the network, our discussion of the case necessarily focuses on its most salient aspects. The dates and key events that correspond to each stage, as well as growth in production and the geographical scope of the network, are summarized in Table 3.2.

Table 3.2 Critical events in the development of the network

	Approximate dates	Key events	Countries entered
Stage 1: opportunity identification	1989–1992	- Karov explores the possibility of selling leather bags and purses to the Russian market. - Karov approaches a Turkish Yugoslavian immigrant who owns a leather factory in Turkey about a possible collaboration.	–
Stage 2: the development of the network	1992–1997	- The two men agree to open a small store in Istanbul (as a joint venture). The store sells a range of leather goods and the products are targeted mainly at Russian tourists. - Karov works hard to build relationships with his Russian customers. The business is very profitable, but Karov realizes he must reach more customers if he is to realize his ambitions. This leads him to expand across a number of Russian cities. He also develops relationships with distributors in Kazakhstan, Byelorussia, Ukraine, and Bulgaria.	Russia, Kazakhstan, Byelorussia, Ukraine, Uzbekistan, and Azerbaijan

	Approximate dates	Key events	Countries entered
Stage 3: leveraging the network	1999–2000	- The distribution network works very well. Karov decides to form his own brand (Neroli) and to source products from a much wider range of manufacturers. - The network expands to 77 stores across Eastern Europe, Russia and its former republics, incorporating around 750 people.	Bulgaria
Stage 4: limits to growth	2000–present	- The network attempts to expand distribution into the US and the UK, but makes little impact. - Network members complain that they lack expertise in key areas such as marketing and finance.	Attempting to enter North America and UK

Stage 1: opportunity identification. Although Karov was able to find a job as a welder, his occupation in Bulgaria before his immigration to Turkey, he was frustrated with the lack of opportunities for immigrants. He noted that:

> The salary I received was barely enough even though I worked as many shifts as possible. I realized that if I remained as an employee in any factory in any position, I would never be able to put my kids through good schools, provide them with good lifestyles. The only option I had was to create something, have my own business...do something on my own.

His frustration led him to go back to Bulgaria and sell his remaining assets in order to raise capital for a potential business. He then traveled throughout Eastern Europe and Russia observing the markets and contemplating his next step. He quickly identified Russia as having the most potential because of its "sophisticated and educated clientele." For a few months at the beginning of 1990, he investigated different options such as exporting pool tables and construction marble. Eventually, however, he noticed a potential business opportunity that he might not have thought of had he not actually visited Russia:

> [I saw] many stylish women on the streets of Moscow carrying their belongings in plastic bags. Not that they wanted to do that, but because they had no option. There were no purses or bags available at that time. ... I saw an opportunity in the market and I acted on it.

Upon his return to Istanbul, he got in touch with a Turkish Yugoslavian acquaintance—Kamal—he had met years ago while vacationing in southern Bulgaria. As we discussed in Chapter 1, Kamal was the owner of Jenni, a moderately successful leather factory manufacturing leather fashion goods (mainly wallets and purses) for the local market. Since Karov was not familiar with the Turkish market and its regulations, and did not have enough capital to start his own business, he asked Kamal if he was interested in jointly opening a small shop in the luggage trade area of Istanbul—an area that was attracting many post-socialist consumers and entrepreneurs. Kamal agreed on the condition that Karov would only own 10 percent of the store and would demand no percentage of the Jenni products sold. Although this does not seem like a very exciting offer in retrospect, it was a great opportunity for an immigrant who had neither capital nor any knowledge of the Turkish market. Karov asked his wife, Aysun, to join him in the store as the majority of the luggage traders were women, and he anticipated that it would be much easier to gain and retain customers if they "worked hand in hand" as husband and wife.

Stage 2: the development of the network. From the beginning, Karov created a special bond with his customers, no matter how small the quantities were that they purchased. For instance, in his first store, there was a sign in Russian and Bulgarian saying, "Please come in for a cup of homeland coffee." This signaled that he and his wife were from the same culture as their Russian and Bulgarian customers. In fact, Aysun confirms that there were many people who only came in for a cup of coffee in the beginning. Karov and Aysun also describe how they would take major customers for dinner and even back to their home for drinks. They mention going for vacations, to birthday parties, and to weddings of their customers. Within six months, Karov had developed relationships with 15 Russian distributors who were selling Jenni products in cities across Russia.

From inception, the transactions between Karov and his Russian customers were based on mutual trust. He allowed his customers to take goods on consignment, sell the products on the streets of Russia, and then bring the money back to Turkey. This flexibility, combined with the strong demand for leather goods in the post-Communist consumer markets, translated into immediate success. Karov claims that not many of the Turkish shop owners trusted Russian customers enough to provide goods in advance. This was mainly because they considered this practice high risk, but also because those store owners did not understand Russian language or culture. Ivan, the main distributor in Russia commented that:

> The luggage trade area at the time consisted of cheap, but bad quality products. People who were coming from Russia to the area would not have much money and that's the type of products they could only demand. Jenni products were ten times more expensive among the leather goods being sold in the area. Not one of the Russian consumers would have been able to buy them if it was not for Karov who trusted us and allowed us to buy the goods in advance. This is how I, like many other customers working with Karov, was able to start business too...Before Karov, I worked with insignificant small shop owners who would never allow me to buy anything in advance.

As the brand became more successful, Karov realized that in order for him to sustain the growth of Jenni, he needed to ensure that the products were sold by competent retailers in shops instead of through street vendors—a decision that was well received by his distribution partners. This proved a crucial step in the network's development, because it established the Jenni brand in the minds of Russian customers. As the brand manager in Moscow explained:

> Jenni was the very first branded leather goods to be sold in the country. It was Karov who put conditions on all of us to open up proper Jenni stores and sell the products in the stores, and not in the street market. I think this was the first step to build the brand and people saw the stores, which immediately signaled that this is a brand name. It is a good quality brand name. Jenni was the first one in the Russian market ... not only in leather goods ... but also as a mere brand itself.

By the end of 1994, Karov had built a profitable network of retail distributors across Russia, but his ambitions did not stop there. In order to build the brand, Karov believed that Jenni needed to broaden the range of products beyond leather goods. The product range was therefore expanded to include bags and belts (sourced mainly from Yugoslavian immigrants living in Turkey).

More significantly, Karov had aspirations beyond Russia and believed that Jenni had potential across Eastern Europe. Once again, he used his shop in the luggage trading area of Istanbul as the focus for his recruitment. He and Aysun made a point of speaking with buyers from the former Soviet Union, building relationships with them, and assessing their trustworthiness and suitability as business partners. They were helped in this respect by the fact that they had the Russian language in common, as well as the shared cultural experiences that came from being non-Russian members of the so-called Eastern Bloc.

The first Jenni stores outside of Russia were opened in two Ukrainian cities—Kiev and Odesa—in the first part of 1994; by the end of 1995 two more Jenni stores had opened in the Ukraine. This was followed by new stores in three more former Soviet countries—Kazakstan, Belarussia, and Kyrgyzstan—which opened during 1996 and 1997.

Stage 3: leveraging the network. The high level of understanding and cooperation between Karov and his partners led to the formation of a highly successful distribution network. Karov used this network to enter the market with his own brand, Neroli, which he created after disagreements with the owners of Jenni about the future of the brand. The owners were reluctant to invest in the brand and expand into more countries. This disagreement between Karov and the owners of Jenni was obvious to many customers. As one customer commented:

> Kemal [the main owner of Jenni] is accidentally a businessman. He is in this business by a complete chance and some other people are making money for him. He is not as driven as us, and does not want to grow his brand or work any harder. He is a 9 to 5 person, who likes to have peace of mind. Unfortunately, this stubbornness or laziness have started to reflect very strongly into the brand... We are still receiving the same exact models of 15–20 years...No innovation whatsoever.

In addition to disagreements about investment and expansion, a further and perhaps more serious issue arose over Karov's wish to take part ownership of the brand, which he believed was justified on the grounds that he had played such a prominent role in its development. The owners of Jenni refused, and this led Karov to create his own business, leveraging his existing contacts and the extensive distribution network he had developed. He subsequently named the new brand after his daughter, Neroli. Karov made two significant changes to Neroli that differentiated it from Jenni. First, the product range included a men's clothing line as well as a range of leather goods. Second, he decided to ensure that the products were of higher quality, and to do this he sought to use Italian suppliers and designers in addition to Turkish ones. The distribution network continued to take on new members, mainly in Russia. In 2000, he expanded into Bulgaria.

Although the two brand names operate in the same market using the same distribution network, their marketing strategies are distinct. Karov is still involved with the Jenni brand and says that he will continue to be because the owners of Jenni helped him when he immigrated to Turkey and, therefore, he owes his success to his former partners. He feels obliged to help them and is still on friendly terms with both the company owners and its managers. Members in the distribution network say they care more about Karov than the Jenni brand and mention they continue to work with that brand only because Karov is still involved. As a Ukrainian distributor said:

> This is not about a brand. It is much more about the people. All my transactions with Jenni brand have always been with Karov and I will not want to work with someone else. If Karov sells X brand, I will have that in my store. If one day, he sells clothes, I will sell that. I trust him. He is a good businessman...Good person.

Stage 4: limits to growth. After just 10 years, the Neroli network—including outsourced production, in-house production, distribution, and retail—grew to incorporate about 750 people and 87 stores in Eastern Europe, Russia, and the former Soviet Republics. However, despite these successes, the reliance on ethnic ties began to inhibit the development of the network in some important respects.

First, most of its partners were from the same ethnic background. Karov said that he does not care about the ethnicity of network members: It is much more important to him that "he or she does the job well, and is an expert." However, he also pointed out the difficulty of finding professionals, especially in accounting and marketing. In addition, he struggled to find a reliable English translator, which has proved a major difficulty as he "only" speaks Russian, Bulgarian, and Turkish. He stresses the fact that not being able to speak English is his

biggest disadvantage and that he would have been much more successful if he had known the language. In his words:

> There are so many opportunities out there but my hands are tied.
> I do not speak English...I cannot do this with a translator. It is
> not the same thing. The translator cannot be as energetic as me,
> or he or she cannot get across what I am trying to say exactly...
> Every mimic, every eye movement...even the tone of the voice has
> a special meaning...My hands are tied without English.

Furthermore, Karov failed in his attempt to expand distribution into
North America through a Moldavian/Russian immigrant based in
Colorado who had seen Neroli products at a trade fair in Moscow. It was
clear from the start that this new member of the network did not have
the capacity to build a strong presence in the US. Similarly, Karov's
recent attempts to source more expensive and sophisticated products,
such as shoes, from his Italian suppliers have foundered due to a range
of cultural and linguistic barriers. And while Karov is keen to expand
into the UK market, he has been unable to build the necessary alliances.

Ethnic ties as enabling new venture formation and success

Neroli's development trajectory from 2000 to 2005 was remarkable.
With limited resources and industry experience, Karov established
the network in nine countries, with combined sales of almost 700,000
units per year. This feat is even more impressive when one takes into
account the backgrounds of network members; like Karov, they were
most often Balkan immigrants who were new to the fashion industry
and had little business experience or personal wealth to draw on. I was
therefore very interested in the relationships, transactions, and patterns of interaction within the network that made this growth possible.

The case analysis revealed three processes that both enabled the
network to expand through new-venture formation and assisted established members in a strategic sense. In the first instance, most obviously, the data suggest that participation in the network allowed
access to resources that might otherwise have been beyond the scope of
members acting autonomously. A second enabling force concerned the
high levels of *trust* exhibited among network members. Particularly
striking was the speed at which trusting relationships developed, as
well as the flexibility they instilled in network relationships. Finally,
a *strategic group identity* emerged as an important asset to network
members. This identity encouraged the shared ethnic experiences and

sense of community, and it established a set of behaviors to which members were expected to conform. In the remainder of this section, we will consider each of these three processes in turn.

Access to resources

The resource advantages of the network were most visible for members at the margins of social and economic activity in their new countries. As noted above, immigrants are often excluded from mainstream labor and capital markets by their lack of knowledge and experience in the workings of their new context and/or by weak linkages with "local" actors. But even where respondents occupied more privileged positions in their adopted homelands, there were clear resource benefits associated with the use of ethnic ties. The resources in question were sometimes financial, taking the form of debt to facilitate the formation or expansion of a venture, asset sharing, or preferential terms and conditions with respect to specialized inputs.

Perhaps more importantly, they also related to knowledge and information about market opportunities or the functioning of a particular market or industry. Longstanding network members who had faced similar or related issues in their entrepreneurial activities were able to pass on the benefits of their experience to others. This was particularly important for knowledge or processes that were complex and had significant tacit components, and were thus difficult to transfer between individuals and/or organizations.

But as Karov's account of his early experiences of working with the Jenni brand illustrates, knowledge transfer was not based on altruism or the assumption that one should help others simply because they are part of the same ethnic group. There are costs associated with searching for partners and transferring assets (Hansen, 1999), costs that are reduced by a reliance on ethnic ties (I expand on this point later in the section). Moreover, the owners of Jenni hoped to capitalize upon Karov's cultural competencies and the possibility of expanding into the Russian market, thereby extending and strengthening their distribution beyond Turkey. In other words, the benefits of asset transfers accrue to asset holders as well as to the network members that acquire the assets.

Trust

The enabling role of ethnic networks extends well beyond resource acquisition and is central to the nature and form of the relationships between actors. This applies not only to the parameters or boundaries of the relationship, but also crucially to the patterns of interaction and modes of behavior among participants. In the context of this study, this manifested itself mainly with respect to the way *trust* was developed and used. Trust is intertwined with conceptions of risk and can be thought of as the "willingness of a party to be vulnerable to the actions of another party, irrespective of the ability to monitor or control that other party" (Mayer, Davis, and Schoorman, 1995: 712).

On several occasions members of the Neroli network exhibited extraordinary trusting behavior; some of the key actors allowed themselves to be exposed to levels of risk that might be considered reckless in "standard" business transactions. In some cases, these risks were mitigated by the fact that the relevant parties were longstanding members of the network who interacted frequently with one another. For example, when it became apparent that distributing merchandise through street vendors was damaging the Jenni brand, Karov approached Ivan, a longstanding business partner, and asked him to set up a flagship store in the heart of Moscow. Ivan was willing to shoulder significant financial risk because he "knew that he [Karov] would not let me down."

At other times, network members engaged in high-risk transactions with actors about whom little was known, confident that their goodwill would be reciprocated but with little or no contractual protection in the event of malfeasance. This was exemplified most obviously by the strategy that Karov employed when seeking to expand into new markets. Rather than asking his partners to purchase stock in advance, he allowed the goods to be paid for *after* they had been sold. This immediately established Karov as a man of integrity and goodwill, and placed the relationship on a solid early footing. It also, of course, created a resource dependency and a sense of obligation that could be used strategically as the relationship developed.

A further benefit was that it allowed a much wider range of potential partners to be included in the network, because vendors were not required to have access to substantial amounts of capital. As noted, relevant industry experience was not necessarily a prerequisite—what mattered was that members felt they could build meaningful and durable relationships with their partners and that they shared an affinity and/or common bond of some kind. The ability to develop these relationships proved to be a crucial strategic advantage for the network as it sought to expand throughout Eastern Europe. Particularly significant was the bond that developed between Russians and Turkish

Bulgarians within the network. Consider the following quotation from a Turkish Bulgarian network member:

> We are very close and get along with Russian people... We have been through communism but not only that... During the communist times, Bulgaria was like 16th republic of Russia... We are born in Bulgaria, and this is where we had our personalities develop. No matter how much of Turkish ethnicity we are, and no matter how long we live in this country, we will never change... We understand where they [Russians] come from, what they want, what they cherish. We have the same integrity.

Strategic group identity

Related to the notion of trust, *strategic group identity* emerged as an important enabling force. Peteraf and Shanley (1997) defined this concept as a "set of mutual understandings" among members of a group, drawing the subtle but crucial distinction between mutual and shared understandings. It is not a prerequisite that members "perceive the group in exactly the same way... [or] mirror each others' characteristics." What matters is that they "understand the behavior of other members and the underlying logic of decision making" (p. 167). This proved vital to the effective functioning of the network that formed the focus of the study because it allowed members to confidently predict the behavior of others without engaging in the repeated transactions normally required in the development of effective relationships. The process of identification also led to the development of shared norms and ways of interacting that facilitated the transfer of knowledge and information within the network. It also imbued it with a robustness based around feelings of togetherness, mutual understanding, and common experience. This suggests a much more complex conception of ethnic identity than is currently espoused in much of the entrepreneurship literature.

Social identification was crucial to the effective functioning of the network in another important respect, because it allowed members who did not conform to group expectations to be "punished" through a process of marginalization. The ability to sanction exhibitions of "improper" behavior in this way provided a powerful incentive for members, especially when combined with the resource dependency described above. It ensured that actions remained within the boundaries of group norms and proved to be an important resource in the absence of contractual protection. This at least partly accounts for why malfeasance was largely absent within the network. As one of the Russian distributors explained:

> We invest almost everything we have for this business. It is our way to upgrade, become successful, and bring some bread to our family...We know that if we cheat, there is no coming back... In fact, when we heard that one of ours had not been paying his money for a while, we all warned him. Because his misbehavior will effect our reputation as Russian customers as well. ...

Ethnic ties as constraining the network

By studying a successful international ethnic network, I expected that the focus of the analysis would be solely on the enabling effects of ethnic ties outlined above and their ramifications for network performance. However—from my perspective somewhat unexpectedly—the study also revealed the constraining effects of these same linkages. These were most apparent when members of the network interacted with prospective members who did not share the same ethic identity. Such interactions tended to occur in circumstances where Neroli was seeking to expand into new markets—markets where it was not always possible to rely upon ethnic ties. The result is that Neroli has a distinctive geography and is concentrated in those countries that are ethnically similar to Balkan immigrants like Karov. Thus, while the firm had been very successful in Russia and large swathes of Eastern Europe, at the time of this study, it had been unable to make inroads into the major international markets across Western Europe and beyond.

Broadly speaking, three processes emerged that inhibited the capacity of the network to enhance its competitive position and acted as constraints on its development. First, *membership lock-in* was found to be an important characteristic of network relations. In this case, individuals were retained within the network even when they had ceased to play a constructive role in its development and/or despite the emergence of a more effective alternative. Second, there was evidence of *over-embeddedness*. This refers to patterns of behavior and interaction that were very entrenched, with the result that network members struggled to respond to deviations from established norms. This meant that relationships with potential partners who were not part of the same ethnic group often became strained as actions and decisions were misinterpreted. The third constraining force was a *lack of competence diversity*. Because the network showed a strong preference for individuals with a shared ethnic heritage and appeared better able to build relationships with them, the network did not always have access to the key skills necessary for effective performance in the leather goods industry.

Membership lock-in

Turning first to *membership lock-in*, I observed that once individuals were accepted into the group, there was a clear reluctance to expunge members who had outlived their usefulness or to switch partners when a more effective alternative emerged. Even when certain members stepped well beyond negotiated group norms and expectations and acted in a way that was clearly detrimental to the network as a whole, expulsion was not always automatic. Of course, even ethnic ties, like all networks, have limits to their tolerance. There were some instances where members were excluded for failing to honor commitments or for impeding network performance. However, this process appeared more drawn out than might be expected in non-ethnic networks where the forces of social identification were less strong.

The most obvious example of lock-in related to Karov's North American distributor. Anton was a US-based businessman who emigrated to America from Bulgaria in 1991; Karov met him at a leather goods fair in Russia at the beginning of 2004. While Anton had no experience in the fashion industry, the two men built a strong relationship based in part on their shared national identity. Karov was convinced that he had found a trustworthy and reliable partner with which to realize Neroli's US ambitions. After just a few weeks, however, Anton's lack of experience in distribution in general, and the leather goods industry in particular, became apparent; he didn't have the competencies, the credibility, or the contacts to establish Neroli in North America. Indeed, Anton was able to sell only a fraction of the $50,000 of stock that had been advanced to him.

In spite of these shortcomings, Karov was very reluctant to break ties with Anton. For Karov the nature of the relationship with partners appeared to be more important that their ability to improve the network's competitive position. For example, in the early stages of their business relations, Karov drew comparisons between Anton's efforts to build a life for his family in the US and his own experiences as an immigrant in Turkey 15 years before. From my perspective, this sense of shared experience dominated the relationship and was at the heart of Karov's unwillingness to sever the link. As Karov noted:

> Anton is an immigrant like me. He knows what it is to struggle in a country that is not your own...where you find it hard to fit in...where you have no other choice other than making money on your own. That's why he has no other choice but be truthful when he does business. This is how I know that he will stay true in our business dealings as well.

Lock-in, of course, is a two-way phenomenon: Not only does it protect modest performance; it also acts to obstruct members who seek to exit the network. The strength of these forces stems in part from the close and trusting nature of the relationships described above. However, there is also the possibility that members who leave the network might become potential competitors. This scenario, in which former members become a significant threat, given their intricate knowledge of network processes and competencies, constitutes a more pragmatic set of motivations.

This form of lock-in was evident on several occasions, most notably in the long and protracted process that ultimately led to Karov's loosening his links with Jenni and starting his own rival brand. Even here, though, the role of ethnicity in the ties that bound him to the management of Jenni was very prominent, as evidenced by the sense of loyalty and responsibility he felt toward them. Although he had wanted to go off on his own for several years, Karov was sensitive to the position of his former employers and agreed to develop a very different brand, to focus on different markets, and to continue to promote Jenni in Russia. According to Karov, "It is an obligation, and a duty that I have to still help them in the Russian market. After all, they were the ones who helped me when I came here to Turkey and had no clue about how things worked."

Over-embeddedness

Bathelt and Taylor (2002) described the second constraining force— *over-embeddedness*—in relation to (non-ethnic) knowledge intensive firms. In particular, they warned against the dangers of very high levels of trust and shared values that had the potential to lead to "blind confidence and gullibility" (p. 102) within networks. In these circumstances, the rules and patterns of interaction that govern behavior become so rigid that they can inhibit the flexibility necessary to respond to changing conditions and contexts.

In the case of Neroli, Karov's reaction to Avi neatly illustrates this phenomenon. Avi was a US businessman who approached Karov in the summer of 2004 with a view to distributing Neroli products across North America. Karov realized that Avi offered tremendous possibilities for Neroli in North America. He had many years of experience in marketing, and his contacts with buyers included some of the largest and most high profile US retailers including Neiman Marcus and Saks Fifth Avenue.

However, a series of requests from Avi halted the relationship in its tracks at an early stage. First, Avi wanted written confirmation that the magnets that Neroli used in its purses and bags would not damage cell phones or other mobile communications technologies. Second, he wanted each of Neroli's products to include a warrantee that customers would receive a replacement or refund in the event of defects in quality. Third, he asked for the weights and dimensions of every Neroli product, as these would be requested by potential buyers. Finally, he asked for exclusive rights to distribute Neroli in the US; this included the termination of Neroli's current arrangement with its existing North American distributor.

From Avi's perspective, such assurances were straightforward. It was reasonable and prudent for him to control for risk in this way, to obtain the kind of information necessary to trade in a litigious society, and to negotiate a strong personal position. From Karov's perspective, however, Avi's approach was not only alien but also contrary to the principles of mutual trust and reciprocity that underpinned his entire strategy for managing network relations. He interpreted Avi's requests as selfish, arrogant, and patronizing. Not only that, but Avi was asking Karov to sever ties with another network member whom he considered a personal friend. Despite its obvious commercial potential, Karov refused to proceed with the partnership.

The process that Karov relies upon to recruit new partners is based upon culturally oriented patterns of interaction. This has proved to be a very effective mode of recruitment for partners with overlapping ethnic identities because both parties are working from a "script" of expected behaviors and are sensitive to the idiosyncrasies of relationship building in that context. Avi, on the other hand, carried a very different set of assumptions about economic transactions and relationship building. In a litigious and consumer-oriented country such as the US, contractual forms of governance operate alongside—and often take precedence over—trust-based ones. Thus, it could be argued that the entrenched nature of Karov's relationship-building routine led him to misinterpret Avi's behavior and fail to appreciate the context within which he was operating.[2]

Lack of competence diversity

Over-embeddedness led in part to a final constraining force: a *lack of competence diversity*. There was a clear tendency for network members to turn to other members when seeking a particular set of competencies—and to be suspicious of individuals who were not part of the same ethnic group. This worked well when the necessary competencies were present within the network. On other occasions the network was poorly served, and its strategic flexibility constrained because of the unwillingness to use non-ethnic partners, even when these partners might have been able to provide specialized inputs more effectively than existing members. As a result, the network was exposed on several occasions, mainly when looking to expand into new markets where the small number of Balkan immigrants made it difficult to leverage ethnic ties.

Neroli's reliance on Anton in the US market, described above, is a clear example of this phenomenon, but there were many others. Indeed, the lack of competence diversity related not only to skills, but also to specialized inputs. This stemmed in part from the difficulties that network members had in developing relationships with individuals and firms that did not share ethnic ties (i.e., over-embeddedness). For example, one of the Russian distributors I interviewed described the difficulties in sourcing goods from Italian suppliers, forcing Neroli to look for suppliers elsewhere. This had significant implications for network competitiveness, as Italian companies tend to produce the best quality products in the leather goods industry. As Karov stated:

> I don't have partners there [in Italy]. It just doesn't happen. It's hard. Italians are the best ones in shoe making, and the Turks can't even come close to them. They have a quality that other producers cannot even reach... But these dealings are not like the ones I have with the Balkan partners... with them it's different. We can talk about particular ideas, concerns and frustrations... they're very flexible [financially], whereas you don't get the same flexibility with Italian businesses.

Moreover, a reliance on ethnic ties led to a shortage of professional labor in accounting and finance, as well as marketing and IT. For instance, the brand manager for Neroli was the daughter of a family friend of another network member. She had no marketing experience, but because her parents had worked in the leather goods industry for many years and been very successful, it was felt that she would quickly learn the necessary skills. According to Karov:

> She is a very young and energetic person who has vision and is willing to work hard. She's never had any similar experience in branding or marketing, but I knew that she must have seen her mother and father managing stores as she was growing up, and that she would be familiar with the business.

Over time, however, it became clear that this individual lacked the necessary skills to manage the brands effectively.

Conclusion: the dynamics of ethnic entrepreneurship

This case study supports Iyer and Shapiro (1999), Light (1972), and Aldrich and Waldinger's (1990) assertion that ethnic groups often struggle to "fit in" to the countries to which they emigrate, in part because of discrimination and in part because of the employment, language, and cultural barriers they encounter. Faced with such conditions, immigrants often look for alternative employment opportunities—and this often involves founding a business venture. However, a lack of financial capital and other resources, as well as inadequate knowledge of local markets and business conventions, leads many immigrants to rely upon ethnic ties to build their venture.

The case also reveals that ethnic entrepreneurship may be far more ambitious and sophisticated than the extant literature suggests. I believe that the depiction of ethnic entrepreneurial ventures as small enterprises exclusively serving similar ethnic needs and tastes is an outdated stereotype. For example, the Neroli case undermines Lerner and Khavul's (2003: 6) assertion that ethnic entrepreneurs "tend to occupy mainly traditional business lines dominated by small firms, and only seldom... grow into larger firms and shift to more advanced and profitable business fields."

With respect to network relations, my analysis suggests that networks based on ethnic ties exert both enabling and constraining forces on members. These forces affect their capacity to combine resources in new ways in order to exploit market opportunities—i.e., their capacity to be entrepreneurial. As is noted below, these forces are not fixed; they may take different forms as the network and its constituent relationships evolve. (See Figure 3.2 for a schematic representation of the enabling and constraining effects of ethnic networks over time.)

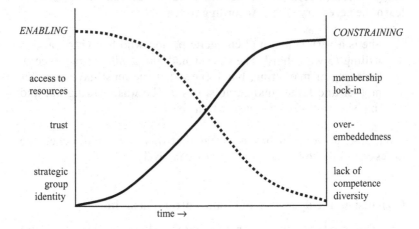

Figure 3.2 A schematic representation of the enabling.

This is an important finding given the current focus on the enabling effects of networks as a strategic resource in the entrepreneurship literature and an almost complete neglect of their "darker side."

As I reflected on the data, it became clear that the enabling and constraining forces within the ethnic network had geographical and temporal components. I can say that, in general, the enabling forces were strongest in the initial stages of network formation and membership. These forces were also strong in places where the network was concentrated in countries with high levels of Balkan immigrants and where access to new contacts and resources played a crucial role in allowing members to build their businesses. Intra-network relationships tended to achieve a high degree of effectiveness relatively quickly, as members capitalized on high levels of trust and their shared strategic identity. As the network matured, the benefits of membership were intertwined with a number of constraints that hindered strategic flexibility. These constraints were not obvious in those locations where there were large numbers of Balkan immigrants but revealed themselves as the network looked to expand further afield.

As Neroli sought to move into Western Europe and North America, it was not always possible to maintain the "ethnic purity" of the network. Yet there was a reluctance to enter into partnerships with people from other ethnic groups, even if they were strategically placed to help Neroli build competitive advantage. Moreover, when relationships with "outsiders" were established, they often faltered as existing members misinterpreted their behavior and decisions. As a result, the network often lacked the competencies to compete effectively beyond the confines of its core markets.

While this study runs against the grain of existing research in entrepreneurship, it is consistent with much of the organizational and sociological research on relationship building in general and networks and social capital in particular. Etzioni (1996), for example, considers that at the core of strong communities of all kinds are boundaries that clearly separate members from non-members. Similarly, Nahapiet and Ghoshal (1998) argue that effective social relations are characterized by "closure" and a strong sense of identity, which necessarily creates boundaries between actors. Should these forces become too strong, however, network interactions run the risk of "producing forms of collective blindness that sometimes have disastrous consequences" (p. 245). Thus it seems that the key strategic issue faced by Neroli—i.e., how to reach beyond its core ties in order to grow while maintaining cohesion and shared purpose—is common to many networks and communities of practice (Brown and Daguid, 2001). In the case of ethnic networks, however, I suggest that this issue is particularly acute because the forces of stasis, path dependence, and embeddedness tend to be stronger.

I recognize, of course, that we must be cautious about these findings and their implications; there are clearly limitations to a study that relies upon a single case over a relatively short period. First, as with all single case studies, there are questions about the generalizability of the results. While the findings seem intuitively appealing, and while they are in many ways consistent with the existing literature, some of the analysis contravenes conventional wisdom. Second, the geopolitical context of the case is unique. While I would argue that this context is helpful for exploring the nature of ethnic entrepreneurship, it is equally possible that, while worthy of study, the specific dynamic of the Neroli network is not representative of ethnic entrepreneurship in general. Finally, the case study takes place over a relatively short period. At one level, this may be construed as a strength, because the key events were fresh in the minds of the respondents, and many documents and other archival data sources were readily accessible. It could also be argued that a longer period is required to understand the complex social processes that were the subject of this investigation. In sum, while I am confident that these findings represent an important step in conceptualizing ethnic entrepreneurship, I do not claim to have produced a definitive account of the dynamics of ethnic networks across space and time.

Notes

1 These figures are based on the estimations in Turkey's Balance of Payments. However, the Central Bank of Turkey estimates those based on surveys with luggage traders at the Ataturk International Airport, Istanbul, Turkey. In 1996, the Central Bank figure was $8.8 billion, dropping to $5.8 billion in 1997. The Central Bank calculated luggage trade exports to be $3.7 billion in 1998 and $2.2 billion in 1999. As the Russian economy gradually stabilized after the August 1998 Russian economy crisis, Turkey's luggage trade earnings slightly recovered in 2000 to $2.9 billion (Yukseker, 2003).
2 Of course, Avi must also take some responsibility for the breakdown of the relationship—he too demonstrated a high degree of tactlessness, but the onus was perhaps on Karov to appreciate the sensitivities of doing business in the US given his ambitions there.

References

Aldrich, H.E. & Waldinger, R. (1990). Ethnicity and entrepreneurship. *Annual Review of Sociology*, 16, 111–135.

Barrett, G., Jones, T., & McEvoy, D. (1996). Ethnic minority business. Theoretical discourse in Britain and North America. *Urban Studies*, 33, 783–809.

Bathelt, H. & Taylor, M. (2002). Clusters, power and place: Inequality and local growth in time-space. *Geografiska Annaler*, 84 B, 93–109.

Bonacich, E. (1973). A theory of Middleman Minorities. *American Sociological Review*, 38, 583–594.

Bonacich, E. & Modell, J. (1980). *The economic basis of ethnic solidarity: small business in the Japanese American Community*. Berkeley: University of California.

Brown, J.S. & Daguid, P. (2001). Knowledge and organization: A social practice perspective. *Organization Science*, 12, 198–213.

Butler, J.S. & Greene, P.G. (1997). Ethnic entrepreneurship: The continuous rebirth of American enterprise. In D.L. Sexton & R.W. Smilor (eds.), *Entrepreneurship 2000*. Chicago: Upstart.

Chaganti, R. & Greene, P.G. (2002). Who are ethnic entrepreneurs? A study of entrepreneurs' ethnic involvement and business characteristics. *Journal of Small Business Management*, 40(2), 126–143.

Dijst, M. & Kempen, R. Van (1991). Minority business and the hidden dimension: the influence of urban contexts on the development of ethnic enterprise. *Tijdschrift voor economische en sociale geografie*, 82, 128–138.

Dyer, L.M. & Ross, C.A. (2000). Ethnic enterprises and their clientele. *Journal of Small Business Management*, 39(2), 48–66.

Eisenhardt, K.M. (1989). Building theories from case study research. *Academy of Management Review*, 14, 532–550.

Etzioni, A. (1996). The responsive community: A communitarian perspective. *American Sociological Review*, 61, 1–11.

Garud, R. & Rappa, M.A. (1994). A Socio-cognitive model of technological evolution: The case of cochlear implants'. *Organization Science*, 5(3), 344–362.

Greve, A. & Salaff, J.W. (2003). Social networks and entrepreneurship. *Entrepreneurship, Theory and Practice*, 28(1), 1–22.

Hansen, M.T. (1999). The search-transfer problem: The role of weak ties in sharing knowledge across organization subunits. *Administrative Science Quarterly*, 44, 82–111.

Iyer, G. & Shapiro, J. (1999). Ethnic entrepreneurial and marketing systems: Implications for the global economy. *Journal of International Marketing*, 7(3), 83–110.

Lerner, M. & Khavul, S. (June 5–7, 2003). Beating the odds in immigrant entrepreneurship: How does founder human capital compare to institutional social capital in improving the survival of immigrant owned businesses? *Paper presented at the Babson Entrepreneurship Conference*, Babson College.

Light, I. (1984). Immigrants and ethnic enterprise in North America. *Ethnic and Racial Studies*, 7, 195–216.

Light, I. (1972). *Ethnic enterprise in America: Business and welfare among Chinese, Japanese and Blacks*. Berkeley: University of California Press.

Light, I. & Bonacich, E. (1988). *Immigrant entrepreneurs*. Berkeley and Los Angeles: University of California.

Light, I. & Gold, S. (eds) (2000). *Ethnic Economies*. San Diego, CA, etc.: Academic Press.

Marger, M.N. & Hoffman, C.A. (1992). Ethnic enterprise in Ontario: Immigrant participation in the small business sector. *International Migration Review*, 26, 968–981.

Mars, G. & Ward, R. (1984). Ethnic business development in Britain: opportunities and resources. In R. Ward and R. Jenkins (eds), *Ethnic communities in business: Strategies for economic survival*, 1–20. London: Cambridge University Press.

Mayer, R.C., Davis, J.H., & Schoorman, F.D. (1995). An integration model of organizational trust. *Academy of Management Review*, 20, 709–734.

Nahapiet, J. & Ghoshal, S. (1998). Social capital, intellectual capital, and the organizational advantage. *Academy of Management Review*, 23, 242–266.

Peteraf, M. & Shanley, M. (1997). Getting to know you: A theory of strategic group identity. *Strategic Management Journal*, Summer Special Issue 18, 165–186.

Pickles, J. (2001). There are no Turks in Bulgaria: Violence, ethnicity, and economic practice in the border regions and Muslim communities of postsocialist Bulgaria. *Mark Planck Institute for Social Anthropology Working Papers*, Working Paper No: 25, Halle/Saale.

Portes, A. (1981). Modes of structural incorporation and present theories of labour immigration. In Kritz, M., Keely, C.B., & Tomasi, S.M. (eds.), *Global trends in migration*. New York: Center for Migration Studies.

Portes, A. & Jensen, L. (1989) The enclave and the entrants: patterns of ethnic enterprise in Miami before and after Mariel. *American Sociological Review*, 54, 929–949.

Simmel, G. (1950). *The sociology of Georg Simmel*. Glencoe: Free Press.

Sowell, T. (1996). *Migration and cultures: A world view*. New York: Basic Books.

Van de Ven, A.H. & Poole, M.S. (1990). Methods for studying innovation development in the Minnesota Innovation Research Program *Organization Science*, 1(3), 313–334.

Waldinger, R., Aldrich, H., & Ward, R. (1990). *Ethnic entrepreneurs: Immigrant business in industrial societies.* Cal.: Sage.

Waldinger, R. (1986). Immigrant enterprise: A critique and reformulation. *Theory and Society*, 15, 249–285.

Wilson, K. & Martin, W.A. (1982). Ethnic enclaves. A comparison of Cuban and Black Economies in Miami. *American Journal of Sociology*, 88, 135–160.

Wilson, K. & Portes, A. (1980). Immigrant enclaves: an analysis of the labor market experience of Cubans in Miami. *American Journal of Sociology*, 86, 295–319.

Yin, R.K. (2003). *Case study research: Design and methods, third edition.* Thousand Oaks, CA: Sage Publications.

Yukseker, D. (2003). *Laleli-Moskova Mekiği: Kayıtdışı Ticaret ve Cinsiyet İlişkileri* [The Laleli-Moscow Shuttle: Informal Trade and Gender Relations]. İstanbul: İletişim Yayınları.

4 Entrepreneurship in emerging markets

Strategies for new venture creation in uncertain institutional contexts

The role of institutions features prominently in the literature on entrepreneurship in emerging markets. For example, Ahlstrom and Brutton (2006: 299) argue that "[e]merging economies are characterized by fundamental and comprehensive institutional transformations as their economies begin to mature." Similarly, Meyer (2001: 358) suggests that "[r]apidly changing institutions may generate, at any point in time, inconsistency between the requirements of different institutions as well as uncertainty over future institutional changes." This body of work has been very useful for understanding the core institutions required for entrepreneurial activity to take place as well as the role that informal structures and practices like family and kinship play in the absence of more formal structures such as laws and regulatory agencies.

An important part of this literature discusses how uncertain institutional contexts in emerging economies *limit* opportunities for entrepreneurship (Luthans and Ibrayeva, 2006). The focus is primarily on how the nature of the institutional environment makes entrepreneurial activity more risky and/or complex. By contrast, in this chapter we will consider how uncertain institutional contexts *create* opportunities for entrepreneurship. Drawing on recent developments in institutional theory, we will explore how a subset of entrepreneurs in emerging markets can exploit institutional uncertainty and create value by solving institutional problems. These entrepreneurs perform various sorts of institutional work (Lawrence and Suddaby, 2006) as they attempt to build businesses in environments characterized by a high degree of institutional uncertainty. In doing so, they often act as *institutional entrepreneurs* (DiMaggio, 1998) whose activities can function as important structuring events that lead emerging markets to become more institutionalized. More specifically, I identify three generic *institutional strategies*—"patterns of action that are concerned with managing the institutional structures within which firms compete for resources" (Lawrence, 1999: 162)—these kinds of entrepreneurs can adopt. These strategies include managing institutional uncertainty, spanning institutional voids, and bridging institutional distance.

These arguments make three important contributions. First, they connect the literature on entrepreneurship in emerging markets (e.g., Ahlstorm and Brutton, 2006) and strategic management in emerging markets (e.g., Hoskisson, Eden, Lau, and Wright, 2000) with recent advances in institutional theory. Over the last decade, institutional theorists have increasingly integrated questions of agency with the traditional concerns of institutional theory such as stability and conformity (e.g., Greenwood and Hinings, 1996; Greenwood, Suddaby and Hinings, 2002). This work is referenced to inform our thinking.

Second, three generic strategies employed by entrepreneurs in emerging markets are identified. There has been a significant amount of work that examines the strategies of multinational corporations (MNCs) in emerging markets (e.g., London and Hart, 2004) and how established firms in emerging markets can respond to MNCs (e.g., Wu and Pangarkar, 2006). However, there has been remarkably little work that examines the strategic options available to entrepreneurs in these contexts (see Peng, 2001 for an exception). I argue that the institutional uncertainty that characterizes emerging markets creates strategic opportunities and that entrepreneurs can capitalize on this uncertainty to create value in various ways.

Third, I provide an alternative theoretical framework for exploring the complex institutional contexts of emerging markets. Although institutional theory has been identified as a potentially useful way of conceptualizing emerging markets, "[t]here is little IT [institutional theory] research on local start-ups in emerging economies" (Wright, Filatotchev, Hoskisson, and Peng, 2005: 9). One of the reasons for this has been the lack of an empirically testable theoretical frame. I have therefore developed a set of testable propositions to help move empirical work forward in this research area. I think this is particularly important, as it allows us to take existing discussions of entrepreneurship in emerging markets in a new direction.

These arguments are presented in four steps. First, there is an overview of the literature on entrepreneurship in emerging markets. Second, we'll discuss the concepts from institutional theory that are useful for understanding entrepreneurship in emerging economies. Third, we'll look at three generic strategies that entrepreneurs in emerging economies can adopt to take advantage of institutional uncertainty. Finally, we'll discuss the implications of these arguments for entrepreneurship theory and consider directions for future research.

Entrepreneurship in emerging markets

Following Hoskisson et al. (2000: 249) I define emerging markets as "low-income, rapid-growth countries using economic liberalization as their primary engine of growth." Thus, not all developing countries can be called emerging markets. Specifically, only those developing countries that (1) undertake a process of economic reform designed to address poverty and improve the living standards of their inhabitants and (2) have an economy that has recorded positive economic growth over a sustained period can "truly" be classified as emerging markets (Cavusgil, Ghauri, and Agarwal, 2002).

There appears to be broad agreement among key scholars (e.g., Arnold and Quelch, 1998; Cavusgil et al., 2002; Hoskisson et al., 2000; Peng, 2003) as well as international development agencies (e.g., World Bank, 2002) that emerging markets include the transition economies of East Asia, Central and Eastern Europe, and the newly independent states of the former Soviet Union, in addition to many of the economies in the Middle East, Latin America, Southeast Asia and Africa. These countries are extremely important, because "approximately 75% of the world's population lives in emerging economies… [and] the population growth rates of emerging economies are the highest of all countries" (Cavusgil et al., 2002: 10).

A notable characteristic of these economies is that the institutions that underpin them are very unstable. Indeed, "[t]he essence of economic transition is the replacement of one coordination mechanism by another. Yet efficient markets depend on supporting institutions that can provide… the formal and informal rules of the game of a market economy" (Meyer, 2001: 358). This process of institutional transformation can produce significant changes over relatively short periods, but the transformation process in its entirety is likely to span many years. For example, during the 1980s, entrepreneurship and competition in the transition economies of the former Soviet Union were unthinkable because of the protected nature of their markets. While this situation has altered dramatically in recent years, "pervasive changes" remain the "striking feature" of these economies (Peng, 2003: 277).

A number of distinct institutional challenges faced by entrepreneurs and firms operating in these contexts have been identified. For example, Peng (2000) distinguishes between formal institutional constraints in emerging markets such as the lack of credible legal frameworks, the lack of stable political structures, and the lack of strategic factor markets. Peng also cites informal institutional constraints such as the prominence of deeply embedded networks and personalized exchanges, both of which make it difficult for "outsiders" to engage in commercial activity. In addition, Cavusgil et al. (2002) argue that a lack of physical infrastructure (e.g., roads, telecommunications, sanitation, and power) and high levels of corruption often represent major barriers for entrepreneurs in emerging economies.

The profound nature of these challenges suggests that the outcome of entrepreneurship in many emerging markets is quite uncertain (Zahra, 1993). In fact, Luthans and Ibrayeva (2006: 93–94) have warned that "rapid and often hostile... political, economic and social changes... are placing unprecedented demands on entrepreneurial functioning" in many emerging markets. More generally, much of the literature has focused on the constraints facing entrepreneurs operating in these contexts.

My argument in this chapter is somewhat different. It is, to some extent, a response to Oliver's (1991: 145) observation that the strategic behaviors that actors use "in direct response to the institutional processes that affect them" have been largely ignored in management studies. Although I recognize that institutional uncertainty poses severe challenges for many entrepreneurs in emerging markets, I also contend that it can create significant opportunities for some entrepreneurs. Yet surprisingly little scholarship considers the ways in which entrepreneurs and other actors exploit institutional uncertainty in order to create wealth. My aim here is to build on recent developments in institutional theory to show how entrepreneurs in emerging markets can also act as institutional entrepreneurs by adopting strategies that exploit uncertainties and contradictions in their institutional environments. Specifically, I am asking the following question: *How do entrepreneurs exploit low levels of institutionalization in emerging markets?*

An institutional perspective on entrepreneurship in emerging markets

Entrepreneurship scholars have increasingly drawn on institutional theory to understand the unique contexts that characterize entrepreneurship in emerging markets. In fact, some authors have argued that institutional theory is *the* most influential and appropriate approach to understanding entrepreneurship in these contexts. "In the early stages of market emergence, institutional theory is preeminent in helping to explain impacts on enterprise strategies" (Hoskisson et al., 2000: 252). Certainly, given the key role that institutions play in building a stable structure for economic activity (Meyer, 2001), the uncertain nature of the institutional arrangements in emerging economies has a powerful impact on entrepreneurial activity.

In this chapter, I draw on neo-institutional theory (e.g., Greenwood and Hinings, 1996; Lounsbury, 2002; Maguire, Hardy, and Lawrence, 2004) and link it to existing discussions of entrepreneurship in emerging markets. Neo-institutional theory is a relatively new perspective that shares much with the institutional approaches that preceded it (e.g., North, 1990; Scott, 1995). However, while previous approaches to studying institutions generally emphasize conformity to institutional norms and/or the embedded nature of behavior, neo-institutional theory looks at institutional change and the role of actors in shaping institutional processes. This makes it a particularly powerful perspective for studying entrepreneurship of different kinds. Moreover, in addition to a concern with formal institutions (such as laws, technologies, and the regulatory environment) that have been the focus of much institutional theory to date, neo-institutional theory also looks at *informal* institutions (such as values, practices, and norms) that have been shown to profoundly affect entrepreneurial behavior (Morris, Davis, and Allen, 1994; Spence, 1985). Neo-institutional theory therefore provides a very effective framework for thinking about the institutional environment of emerging markets.

Institutions and institutional uncertainty

At the broadest level, institutions are self-policing conventions (Douglas, 1986). Institutions influence behavior because deviation from the accepted institutional order is costly in some way. For example, institutions such as standard business practices, technological standards, industry codes of practice, and standard contracts all impose powerful constraints on strategic decision making. In addition, the more highly institutionalized a particular social pattern is, the more costly such deviations are (Lawrence, Winn, and Jennings, 2001). Institutions contain mechanisms that associate non-conformity with increased costs in several different ways: "economically (it increases risk), cognitively (it requires more thought), and socially (it reduces legitimacy and the access to resources that accompany legitimacy)" (Phillips, Lawrence, and Hardy, 2000: 28).

An important dimension of this view of institutions is that institutionalization is not a binary concept; institutions cannot be characterized only as existing or not existing. Rather, institutionalization is on a continuum, and the result is a gradation of levels of institutionalization accompanied by associated mechanisms of self-reinforcement (Maguire et al., 2004). Specifically, institutionalization varies from weakly institutionalized, with minimal costs associated with deviation, to very deeply institutionalized, with significant costs associated with deviation; it is therefore not all-or-nothing but rather a matter of degree.

This has clear ramifications for economic activity in emerging markets. The challenges facing entrepreneurs in emerging markets do not simply stem from the fact that particular structures are not in place; it may also be the case that those institutions that are in place are not deeply institutionalized. "Proto-institutions"—that is, new practices, rules, and technologies that become available inter-organizationally and that may become fully fledged institutions if they diffuse sufficiently (Lawrence, Hardy and Phillips, 2002)—may exist. These, however, have not yet developed the self-reinforcing mechanisms that encourage predictable patterns of behavior and hence reduce risk. This low degree of institutionalization results in a high degree of uncertainty and requires careful responses from potential entrepreneurs.

In sum, the continuum of institutionalization varies from an almost complete absence of particular institutions (as in parts of developing countries), to environments that are highly institutionalized (as in parts of developed countries). Moreover, in addition to these polarities, many institutional spaces in emerging economies are populated by more-or-less institutionalized proto-institutions, which, while they have some influence on behavior and have the potential to become institutions, are only weakly entrenched.

Organizational fields and entrepreneurial opportunities

Given that different parts of emerging economies develop and institutionalize at different rates, an important question is how these distinctive institutional spaces should be treated. In neo-institutional theory, the focus has been on groups of organizations that share sets of institutions. This level of analysis has been conceptualized as the organizational field.[1] An organizational field is defined as:

> [T]hose organizations that, in the aggregate, constitute a recognized area of institutional life: key suppliers, resource and product consumers, regulatory agencies, and other organizations that produce similar services or products. The virtue of this unit of analysis is that it directs our attention not simply to competing firms... or to the networks of organizations that actually interact...but to the totality of relevant actors.
>
> (DiMaggio and Powell, 1983: 148)

Crucially, actors involved in a recognizable area of institutional life have a sense of being part of a common activity with other field members. Actors outside the field will also often recognize that this group of organizations has a particular identity and will be able to identify the boundary of the organizational field.

DiMaggio and Powell argue that organizational fields comprise three core components. The first component—institutions—was discussed above. The second component is a network of organizations (Hinings and Greenwood, 1988). These networks are not simply aggregates of organizations, however, but patterned relationships that disseminate power and resources among the members of the field (Bourdieu, 1993; Fligstein, 1996). Finally, fields are characterized by particular configurations of resources that result from these patterned interactions and that are distributed unevenly among the various actors.

In the literature, scholars have made the distinction between mature and emerging fields. Mature fields are characterized by stable and ordered exchanges between participants and high levels of mutual awareness with respect to the actors that are included and excluded from particular institutional practices (Greenwood and Suddaby, 2006). By contrast, emerging fields are characterized by loosely coupled networks of actors with few widely diffused rules and practices (Maguire et al., 2004). As the participants seek to build new understanding and produce new institutional arrangements, their interests and identities are necessarily unstable and ill-defined (Fligstein, 2001).

The development of new organizational fields is a key feature of economic activity in emerging markets. This presents entrepreneurs with two opportunities: They can take advantage of the uncertainty this creates to establish new businesses, and/or they can play a key role in the development of organizational fields by influencing the processes of institutionalization. In other words, entrepreneurs in emerging markets have the potential to act as *institutional entrepreneurs*.

Institutional entrepreneurship in emerging markets

Institutional entrepreneurship—"the activities of actors who have an interest in particular institutional arrangements and who leverage resources to create new institutions or to transform existing ones" (Maguire et al., 2004: 657)—has been the focus of increasing interest among institutional theorists (e.g., Garud, Jain, and Kumaraswamy, 2002; Greenwood et al., 2002; Lounsbury, 2002). The activities of institutional entrepreneurs have come to be seen as a key source of change in mature fields (e.g., Greenwood and Suddaby, 2006), while in emerging fields they are also considered crucial to the process by which fields become stable and established (e.g., Maguire et al., 2004). In both cases, institutional entrepreneurship has been an important route to connecting institutional theory with questions of agency and intention, as interested individuals work to establish their interests in the organizational fields of which they are a part. "New institutions arise when organized actors with sufficient resources (*institutional entrepreneurs*) see in them an opportunity to realize interests that they value highly" (DiMaggio, 1988: 14).

Institutional entrepreneurship is an important concept because it highlights the ways in which actors work toward their strategic objectives; these actors *deliberately* leverage resources (cognitive, social, and material) in order to create and/or manipulate the institutional structures in which they are embedded (Lawrence, 1999; Dorado, 2005). Garud et al. (2002: 196–197), for example, argue that "[a]ssuming the role of champions... [institutional entrepreneurs] energize efforts towards collective action and devise strategies for establishing stable sequences of interaction with other organizations" in order to create new institutional configurations.

Given the high levels of uncertainty, institutional entrepreneurship in emerging markets is liable to involve a different set of skills than those associated with institutional entrepreneurship in established markets. This is due to the fact that much of the institutional landscape in emerging markets is made up of organizational fields that are indistinct and relatively poorly institutionalized. A key aspect of institutional entrepreneurship in emerging economies is the capacity of actors to build networks and alliances and to legitimatize new sets of practices among other key actors as organizational fields take shape. For example, Mcmillan and Woodruff (2002: 161) found that "gossip" in Vietnam's manufacturing community allowed firms to gather information about trading partners from other firms "by spreading information about who had breached contracts and coordinating the sanctioning of them." The result was that malfeasance "brought more severe consequences than merely losing the business of the offended party and thus increased the likelihood of cooperation."

Maguire et al. (2004) argue that institutional entrepreneurs in emerging fields tend to (1) have identities and roles that allow them to build legitimacy and access resources amongst diverse stakeholders; (2) have the ability to develop lines of argument that appeal to diverse stakeholders and the political skills to build stable coalitions among them; and (3) are able to make connections between existing organizational practices and the new practices and align the new practices with the values of key stakeholders. In a similar vein, other institutional theorists have emphasized the importance of relationships and the capacity to build legitimacy among diverse stakeholders as crucial to institutional entrepreneurship in emerging fields. The analysis by Garud et al. (2002) of Sun Microsystem's sponsorship of its Java technology clearly showed the importance of managing legitimacy across multiple stakeholders in emerging fields.

Institutional strategies in emerging markets

In the previous section, we discussed how some entrepreneurs in emerging markets create ventures that exploit institutional uncertainty. One way to understand the activities of these entrepreneurs is to conceptualize them as following "institutional strategies."

> Institutional strategies are patterns of organizational action concerned with the formation and transformation of institutions, fields and the rules and standards that control those structures. Although all organizational strategy occurs within an institutional context, institutional strategy is differentiated by its orientation to that context: simply put, institutional strategy is not so much concerned with gaining competitive advantage based on existing institutional structures as it is concerned with managing those structures—preserving or transforming institutional standards and rules in order to establish a strategically favorable set of conditions.
>
> (Lawrence, 1999: 167)

Thus, institutional strategies involve managing the institutional context in order to gain competitive advantage. For entrepreneurs in emerging markets, this means working to affect the organizational field in which they wish to found their new ventures in a way that allows them to create value. As we discussed above, fields characterized by relatively low levels of institutionalization pose severe challenges for traditional entrepreneurship. The creation of new ventures without formal institutions, such as functioning laws and regulatory frameworks, involves high levels of risk and complexity (Peng, 2001). If there is also a lack of informal institutions, like shared industry norms and common business practices, then this only adds to the risk.

In these circumstances, I suggest that entrepreneurs increasingly turn to institutional strategies to create value, in part because there is more opportunity to do so and in part because it is more necessary to do so. The opportunities stem from the high levels of institutional uncertainty in emerging markets; as uncertainty increases there are more and more ways to create businesses. Similarly, the absence of critical institutions increasingly requires entrepreneurs to act as institutional entrepreneurs.

Thus, in the face of high levels of institutional uncertainty, entrepreneurs may be forced to act as institutional entrepreneurs if they wish to build successful businesses. This reasoning leads to my first proposition:

> *P1: As institutional uncertainty increases, the likelihood of entrepreneurs following institutional strategies increases.*

In the remainder of this section, we will explore the kinds of institutional strategies that entrepreneurs can follow in conditions of institutional uncertainty. Building on the previous discussion of institutional theory, the literature on strategy in emerging markets, and the literature on institutional strategies, I propose that there are three generic institutional strategies available to entrepreneurs in emerging markets: managing institutional uncertainty, spanning institutional voids, and bridging institutional distance (see Table 4.1). In the following three subsections we will consider each strategy in turn.

Table 4.1 Generic institutional strategies

Institutional strategy	Description
1 Manage institutional uncertainty	Entrepreneurs following this strategy to create value by helping to reduce the institutional uncertainty faced by members of an organizational field to which they do not belong. In doing so, the entrepreneur reduces risk, increases certainty, and facilitates economic activity in the field.
2 Span institutional voids	Entrepreneurs following this strategy create value by building proto-institutions in areas of the economy that are characterized by low degrees of institutionalization and then diffusing them across the organizational field. In doing so, they become a central actor in the field and help to structure the field.
3 Bridge institutional distance	Entrepreneurs following this strategy create value by transposing institutions from another national context into an emerging market. This often requires substantial modification for the institution to function effectively in the local environment.

Managing institutional uncertainty

The first institutional strategy involves entrepreneurs founding ventures that reduce the institutional uncertainty faced by other actors in a particular organizational field. In doing so, entrepreneurs create value by moderating the risk of economic transactions. The introduction of institutions that reduce uncertainty plays a key role in emerging markets, because these institutions form the building blocks of market-based economic activity. Peng (2001) notes that entrepreneurs who reduce uncertainty in this way are entrepreneurs in the classical sense of the term because they perform a brokerage role. Specifically, "they blur the boundaries separating different sectors by taking advantage of the information and resource asymmetries across sectors" (p. 96).

I believe that there are two important requirements for this strategy to be successful. First, the business model that the entrepreneur develops must reduce the institutional uncertainty faced by a second party in a way that the second party could not easily do itself. This second party might be a foreign company seeking to do business in an unfamiliar environment or a local firm or individual without the knowledge or connections required to manage its institutional environment independently.

Alternatively, there may be advantages to grouping transactions from several actors and facilitating their completion in a way that none of them could achieve individually. For instance, the complex networks of "hawala" or "hundi" money transfer in southern Asia (Buencamino and Gorbunov, 2002), which involve many small businesses organizing international money transfer, is an example of a new organizational form created by entrepreneurs that reduces institutional uncertainty for their customers in emerging markets. Over time, this practice has become highly institutionalized in particular geographic areas.

Second, the business model developed by the entrepreneurs must enable them to appropriate some of the wealth they generate for their partners. Simply reducing the institutional uncertainty faced by others is not sufficient; the entrepreneur needs to develop a strategy for capturing a proportion of the value they help to create in a consistent and sustainable way. For example, in Russia, it is common for international entrepreneurs to work through a local distributor or intermediary who manages the local environment on the entrepreneurs' behalf (Karra, Tracey and Phillips, 2006). Most notably, those intermediaries that manage the very sensitive and risky problems of personal and company security and that interface with government officials to organize licensing and taxation issues provide a valuable service to entrepreneurs in emerging markets. Generally, it is common practice for intermediaries to take possession of merchandise and then sell it for a profit.

In many cases, the local intermediary knows little about the core business that he or she is involved in. However, through complex webs of relationships and deep local knowledge, the local partner can make sense of the institutional environment for their international partner and, in turn, generate substantial revenues for both parties.

Managing institutional uncertainty is a critical issue in emerging markets (Peng, 2002) and can therefore create significant opportunities for entrepreneurs. The high degree of institutional uncertainty faced by individuals and organizations in these environments presents a real opportunity for entrepreneurs who can identify ways to reduce this uncertainty. Furthermore, the greater the uncertainty faced by members of the field, the greater the opportunities presented to entrepreneurs to manage it. This leads to the second proposition:

> *P2: The greater the degree of institutional uncertainty in an organizational field, the greater the likelihood that entrepreneurs will seek to manage this uncertainty.*

In other words, the greater the degree of institutional uncertainty in an organizational field, the more opportunity provided entrepreneurs to adopt this institutional strategy and the more we would expect this strategy to become a common entrepreneurial approach.

Spanning institutional voids

The notion of an institutional void has recently appeared in management studies and international business. For example, in the management literature, Hensmans (2003: 366) defines institutional voids as "political spaces of legitimation unarticulated by incumbent archetypes." In the context of international business, Khanna and Palepu (2006: 62) use the term to refer to "the absence of specialist intermediaries, regulatory systems, and contract-enforcing mechanisms" in an economy. Building on Khanna and Palepu (2006), we can see that an institutional void refers to the relative absence of the institutions that facilitate business transactions as well as the absence of an associated set of rewards and sanctions to enforce those rules, norms, and belief systems.

Creating institutions that span these institutional voids is a challenging form of institutional entrepreneurship. As noted above, an organizational field is composed of a set of institutions and a network of organizations; in an institutional void neither the institutions nor the network is well developed. This causes two problems for entrepreneurs. First, the interests and identities of the key actors are very unstable (Fligstein, 2001). It is not clear who the key actors will be or what roles they will adopt. Thus, for entrepreneurs wishing to create new ventures to span these voids, it is difficult to ascertain the key actors with whom they need to engage or to determine how to relate to them.

Furthermore, as institutional voids are unstructured institutional spaces, they do not contain a defined and widely shared set of institutions. Thus, there are no commonly accepted business practices, organizational structures, dominant designs, industry standards, or other types of institutions that characterize more developed organizational fields. This means that spanning institutional voids is likely to involve high levels of ambiguity and to be characterized by a combination of intended and unintended consequences.

The objective for entrepreneurs working to span institutional voids is that their approach to solving a given institutional problem become the standard and accepted one within the emerging field. In order to fill these voids, entrepreneurs need to build networks and alliances and to legitimatize new institutions among relevant actors (Maguire et al., 2004). While this can be a difficult task, entrepreneurs wishing to create businesses within institutional voids have little choice but to follow this institutional strategy. More conventional approaches to new venture creation are unlikely to succeed in an institutional void because of the lack of stable and predictable institutions and networks that facilitate conventional economic transactions (Khanna and Palepu, 2006).

However, entrepreneurs do not simply produce a full-fledged institution; they first create a proto-institution and make it available to other actors (Lawrence et al., 2002). Once they have created the proto-institution and made it available, it will need to be widely adopted by key participants in the new field for it to become institutionalized. Thus, entrepreneurs need to educate other actors about the skills and knowledge required to support the new institution (Lawrence and Suddaby, 2006). This second stage is considerably more difficult than the first: while proto-institutions are usually the result of intended actions, the embedding process is much less predictable and more difficult to control (Lawrence et al., 2002). Unintended consequences are thus an inevitable feature of this part of the institutionalization process (Lawrence and Phillips, 2004).

The Grameen Bank provides an interesting example of the way entrepreneurs in emerging markets can span institutional voids. The entrepreneur who created it, Muhammad Yunus, realized that there was no mechanism for the rural poor in Bangladesh to access capital because they didn't have any collateral. In response, he created an alternative banking system based on trust and community support—one that involved risk shared among community members. Then, in order to make this formal institution work, he had to support the development of an associated set of norms and practices.

The bank began as a localized activity in the Tangail district of Bangladesh in 1979. However, it has since expanded across most of the country; by 2006, it had 6.7 million borrowers spread over 86 percent of the villages in Bangladesh. In addition, the bank has become a model for microlending in countries all around the world.

Thus, I suggest that a key strategy employed by institutional entrepreneurs in emerging markets involves spanning institutional voids. By creating new institutions and corresponding sets of rewards and sanctions to support them, entrepreneurs can exploit undeveloped institutional spaces in order to generate wealth-creating opportunities. While this strategy is also used by entrepreneurs in well-developed organizational fields, I argue that it will be particularly prominent in emerging markets. This leads to the following proposition:

> *P3: The less institutionalized an institutional void, the greater the likelihood that entrepreneurs will seek to create wealth by building new institutions.*

In sum, for entrepreneurs seeking to create new ventures within institutional voids, traditional approaches to entrepreneurship are not viable because of the absence of the key institutions and networks of actors required for economic activity to take place. In these circumstances, entrepreneurs need to create new institutions, both formal and informal, in order for their ventures to succeed.

Bridging institutional distance

The third institutional strategy available to entrepreneurs in emerging markets is *bridging institutional distance*. In international business, institutional distance has been used to conceptualize the challenges faced by MNCs seeking to establish operations in different countries. It has been defined as the extent to which the institutions in the home and host countries differ from one another (Kostova, 1999). This literature has focused in particular on two strategic issues (Xu and Shenkar, 2002): (1) the barriers faced by MNCs in building legitimacy in their host country and (2) the barriers faced by MNCs when transferring organizational practices from the parent company to the subsidiary in the host country. Kostova and Zaheer (1999) argue that the greater the institutional distance between home and host countries, the more difficult it becomes for MNCs to build legitimacy and transfer practices. In their words: "In other words, a large institutional distance triggers the conflicting demands for external legitimacy (or local responsiveness) in the host country and internal consistency (or global integration) within the MNC system" (Xu and Shenkar, 2002: 610).

In the context of entrepreneurship in emerging markets, I conceptualize bridging institutional distance as the practice of translating (Sahlin-Anderson, 1996) or transposing (Boxenbaum and Battilana, 2005) institutions between countries. Most obviously, this involves transferring institutions from a developed economy in order to exploit an emerging market. Neroli—the company we studied in Chapters 2 and 3—implanted this strategy in Russia. In the mid-1990s, Ishmael Karov, Neroli's CEO, transferred the concept of the specialized menswear store from North America and Western Europe to Russia. Prior to this, clothing in Russia had been sold mainly in large state department stores or in street markets. Karov successfully implemented this strategy by adapting the Western concept of a menswear store to the realities of the Russian context. This successful example of institutional bridging was part of the rapid transformation of clothing retailing that occurred in Russia following the liberalization of the economy in the early 1990s.

In Soviet Russia, consumer goods were generally of poor quality and in short supply. There were several reasons for this. Government planners tended to concentrate on heavy industry, military hardware, and the space race. In addition, there was the doctrine held by many communist party leaders that a focus on consumer goods was simply undesirable (it was seen as imitating capitalist economies). Finally, there was a disconnect between supply and demand. All requests for products from government-owned department stores had to go through the bureaucracy in Moscow—a lengthy process.

The Soviet economy was *deeply institutionalized*—but the institutions were not providing consumers with the products they wanted—or in the quantity they wanted. Consumer goods were mostly sold at large government department stores; long queues often formed when new products came in. The end result was a thriving black market and a pent-up desire on the part of consumers for quality products.

When the Soviet institutions began to break down, the economy transitioned from a highly institutionalized planned economy into an emerging free market economy in just a few short years. The resulting *institutional uncertainty*, combined with the pent-up demand for quality goods, provided fertile ground for many shrewd entrepreneurs.

But bridging institutional distance might also involve transferring institutions between organizational fields in two emerging economies. For example, the concept of developing businesses that deliver very low-cost products and services to consumers at "the bottom of the pyramid" (Prahalad, 2004), pioneered by entrepreneurs in Brazil, is increasingly used as a strategy by entrepreneurs in India, China, and other emerging markets. These entrepreneurs take advantage of the immense collective buying power of low-income consumers to sell products like personal computers. Thus, business models designed for consumers in emerging markets are increasingly being transferred to other emerging markets through a form of institutional bridging.

Moreover, institutional bridging need not be confined simply to the introduction of a new organizational form from one context to another; it might also involve the transfer of a set of organizational practices, norms, technologies, or any other form of institution. For

---

In 1969, Dr. Karsanbhai Patel, a chemist in the town of Ruppur, India (state of Gujarat), began to manufacture a new kind of detergent powder. Patel would bicycle 15 km to work every day and, on his way, he would sell 15 to 20 packets of the detergent to low-income households. Because the new powder sold for a quarter of the price of commercial detergents—and was delivered to the door—it caught on very quickly. Patel started packing the powder in a small room in his house under the name of Nirma.

By 1985, Nirma had become a popular detergent in many parts of the country. By 1999, Nirma was a major national brand offering soaps and personal care products as well as detergent. Nirma had 400 distributors and two million retail outlets—many in very small villages. By continuing to market to low-income households, the company grew quite large.

This bottom-of-the-pyramid success caught the eye of MNCs such as Hindustan Lever Ltd. (HLL), a subsidiary of Great Britain's Unilever. Impressed by the rapid growth of Nirma, HLL introduced its own low-priced line of detergents and consumer care products. The success of this line, which now competes successfully with the Nirma products, underscores the tremendous purchasing power of consumers at the bottom of the income pyramid.

example, Chandra and Devanath (2003) describe how an Indian dairy cooperative adapted supply chain practices from the dairy industry in the US, New Zealand, and Denmark in order to overcome the fragmented nature of the Indian dairy market. These practices included building trust, transferring innovation, and developing systems of coordination among suppliers. This "revolution" in the Indian dairy industry has led to the emergence of India as one of the largest global producers of milk.

Entrepreneurs that bridge institutional distance might belong to the country into which the new institution is being transferred, the country from which the institution is being transferred, or perhaps even a third country. However, in each case it is crucial that they have a deep understanding of the "home" and "host" contexts; not all entrepreneurs are equally likely or able to transfer institutions (Boxenbaum, 2006). Multiple embeddedness is a key condition that enables individuals to transpose institutions between jurisdictions (Sewell, 1992). This is because bridging institutional distance is a complex task, and some institutions may be extremely difficult to translate even if they have been very effective in another organizational field. Indeed, Biggart and Guillén (1999: 726) note that "even countries wishing to adopt... practices presumed to be most efficient or effective can incorporate only those that 'make sense' to the actors being organized."

Deep knowledge of the home and host contexts allows entrepreneurs to assess (1) whether a given institution has the potential to be transposed effectively and (2) the extent to which a given institution will need to be altered in order to "fit" the new context. I therefore suggest that bridging institutional distance represents a third generic strategy available to entrepreneurs in emerging markets. This leads to the next proposition:

P4: The greater the institutional distance between the home and host contexts, the more entrepreneurs in emerging markets are required to act as institutional entrepreneurs when transposing institutions.

Clearly, the greater the institutional distance between the contexts being bridged, the more difficult and risky it will be for entrepreneurs in emerging markets to transpose a given institution and create a new organizational field (Kostova and Zaheer, 1999). Thus, the tension between local legitimacy and internal consistency, outlined above in the context of MNC investment, is liable to feature prominently when entrepreneurs seek to bridge institutional distance. Indeed, for small institutional distances, it is likely that a given institution can be transferred directly between fields. For larger distances, it is likely that the entrepreneur will need to adapt a given institution so that it fits with the host context.

However, while risk increases as the institutional distance increases, the potential rewards also increase; because bridging large institutional distances is more complex, it is also less subject to the forces of standardization and imitation. Developing a product or service that is more difficult to replicate or copy will lead to significantly higher levels of value being created (Alvarez and Busenitz, 2001). These lines of reasoning lead to the following propositions:

> *P5-A: Increased institutional distance between the home and host contexts leads to increased risk for entrepreneurs following a bridging strategy.*
>
> *P5-B: Increased institutional distance between the home and host contexts leads to increased rewards for entrepreneurs who successfully transpose institutions following a bridging strategy.*

In other words, increasing institutional distance leads to both increased risk and reward; when transposing institutions becomes more and more difficult, the potential payoff from success grows too. This, of course, raises questions about the sorts of circumstances under which the reward may grow faster than the risk leading to increased levels of this activity.

Conclusions

In this chapter, I have argued that while the high degree of institutional uncertainty that characterizes emerging markets often acts as a barrier to entrepreneurship, it can also provide important opportunities for entrepreneurs. Building on insights from neo-institutional theory, I have developed a framework for understanding the activities of entrepreneurs who exploit this uncertainty. I have framed this kind of entrepreneurship as a form of institutional entrepreneurship. In this framework, the entrepreneur develops an "institutional strategy" (Lawrence, 1999) in order to exploit aspects of an emerging organizational field to create value. Specifically, I have proposed three generic institutional strategies available to entrepreneurs in emerging markets: managing institutional uncertainty, spanning institutional voids, and bridging institutional distance. I have also proposed conditions under which these forms of entrepreneurship are more likely to occur. These arguments make three significant contributions. First, they connect the literature on entrepreneurship in emerging markets with relevant literature on strategy in emerging markets and neo-institutional theory. This combination provides a theoretical frame to examine the purposeful strategies of entrepreneurs in emerging markets. Second, I have argued that the institutional uncertainty that characterizes emerging organizational fields can provide significant opportunities for entrepreneurs. This is an important insight because it enables us to conceptualize three generic institutional strategies that entrepreneurs can adopt to exploit these uncertainties. Finally, and perhaps most important, is the introduction of neo-institutional theory as a framework for considering the distinctive nature of emerging market economies. Neo-institutional theory offers a more balanced view of institutions than earlier forms of institutional theory, in part because it highlights both formal and informal institutional processes and focuses on strategic action by purposeful actors. For these reasons, I consider it to provide a better foundation for research in the area.

The above discussion highlights three important areas for further research. First, there is a need for more research and theoretical investigation into how the institutional context shapes entrepreneurial strategies in emerging economies. As noted above, there has been some work discussing how institutional uncertainty creates barriers to entrepreneurial activity. However, while the existing work is interesting and helpful, much more work is needed to explain exactly how institutional uncertainty shapes entrepreneurial activity in emerging economies.

Second, there is a need for additional work examining the entrepreneurial capabilities that underpin success in the kinds of institutional strategies covered in this chapter. There has been considerable research on entrepreneurial capabilities—"the ability to identify a new opportunity and develop the resource base needed to pursue the opportunity" (Arthurs and Busenitz, 2006: 199)—that lead to success in traditional entrepreneurship. While some of the entrepreneurial capabilities identified in the entrepreneurship literature seem intuitively appealing, presumably additional capabilities are critical to success for institutional entrepreneurship in emerging economies. I suggest that more work needs to be done to identify the key entrepreneurial capabilities that underpin this kind of entrepreneurship.

Finally, the role of entrepreneurs in structuring organizational fields in emerging markets is a fascinating research topic with important ramifications for our understanding of entrepreneurship and emerging economies and even for theories of economic development. I have suggested that the actions of entrepreneurs can have important and lasting consequences, as described in the following passage:

> In new fields, institutional entrepreneurs are engaged in emergent, contingent strategies, where their initial choices lead to unintended and unexpected consequences to which they then adapt. At the same time, early followers are relatively blindly imitating the choices of those institutional entrepreneurs out of a desire for certainty and legitimacy. Consequently, emerging institutional structures that define the field are highly vulnerable to the initial decisions of institutional entrepreneurs as well as the early influences of customers and other stakeholders.
>
> (Lawrence and Phillips, 2004: 707)

In Lawrence and Phillips' (2004) study, the entrepreneurs who initially established the field set its tone and direction despite the fact that many of their decisions were arbitrary and based on convenience or personal preferences rather than rational choice. In other words, the actions of entrepreneurs in emerging markets have the potential to drive processes of institutionalization. However, this aspect of entrepreneurship in emerging markets has been largely overlooked. Much more theorizing and empirical investigation is required to enhance our understanding of this important dynamic.

Note

1 At least three different terms are used interchangeably in the literature—organizational field (e.g., DiMaggio and Powell, 1983), interorganizational field (e.g., Leblebici et al., 1991), and institutional field (e.g., Phillips et al., 2000). I will use the term organizational field in this chapter.

References

Ahlstrom, D. & Brutton, G.D. (2006). Venture capital in emerging economies: Networks and institutional change. *Entrepreneurship: Theory and Practice*, 30(2), 299–320.

Alvarez, S. & Busenitz, L. (2001). The entrepreneurship of resource-based theory. *Journal of Management*, 27, 755–775.

Arnold, D.J. & Quelch, J.A. (1998). New strategies in emerging markets. *Sloan Management Review*, Fall, 40, 7–20.

Arthurs, J. D. & Busenitz, L. W. (2006). Dynamic capabilities and venture performance: The effects of venture capitalists. *Journal of Business Venturing*, 21(2), 195–215.

Biggart, N.W. & Guillen, M.F. (1999). Developing difference: Socialorganization and the rise of the auto industries of South Korea, Taiwan, Spain, and Argentina. *American Sociological Review*, 64, 722–747.

Bourdieu, P. (1993). *Sociology in question*. London: Sage.

Boxenbaum, E. & Battilana, J. (2005). Importation as innovation: Transposing managerial practices across fields. *Strategic Organization*, 3, 355–383.

Boxenbaum, E. (2006). Lost in translation: The making of Danish diversity management. *American Behavioral Scientist*, 49, 939–948.

Buencamino, L. & Gorbunov, S. (2002). Informal money transfer systems: Opportunities and challenges for development finance. *Discussion Paper of the United Nations Department of Economic and Social Affairs*, No. 26.

Cavusgil, T., Ghauri, P., & Agarwal, M. (2002). *Doing business in emerging markets: Entry and negotiation strategies*. Thousand Oaks: Sage.

Chandra, P. & Devanath, T. (April, 2003). *Business strategies for managing complex supply chains in large emerging economies: The story of AMUL*. Working Paper. Institute of Management, Ahmedabad, India.

DiMaggio, P.J. & Powell, W.W. (1983). The iron cage revisited: Institutional isomorphism and collective rationality in organizational fields. *American Sociological Review*, 48, 147–160.

DiMaggio, P.J. (1988). Interest and agency in institutional theory. In L.G. Zucker (ed.), *Institutional patterns and organizations: Culture and environment*, 3–21. Cambridge, MA: Ballinger.

Dorado, S. (2005). Institutional entrepreneurship, partaking and convening. *Organization Studies*, 26, 385–414.

Douglas, M. (1986). *How institutions think*. Syracuse: Syracuse University Press.

Fligstein, N. (1996). Markets as politics: A political-cultural approach to market institutions. *American Sociological Review*, 61, 656–673.

Fligstein, N. (2001). *The architecture of markets: An economic sociology of twenty-first-century capitalist societies*. Princeton: Princeton University Press.

Garud, R., Jain, S., & Kumaraswamy, A. (2002). Institutional entrepreneurship in the sponsorship of common technological standards: The case of Sun Microsystems and Java. *Academy of Management Journal*, 45, 196–214.

Greenwood, R. & Hinings, C.R. (1996). Understanding radical organizational change: Bringing together the old and the new institutionalism. *Academy of Management Review*, 21, 1022–1054.

Greenwood, R. & Suddaby, R. (2006). Institutional entrepreneurship in mature fields: The big five accounting firms. *Academy of Management Journal*, 49, 27–48.

Greenwood, R., Suddaby, R., & Hinings, B. (2002). Theorizing change: the role of professional associations in the transformation of institutionalized fields. *Academy of Management Journal*, 45, 58–80.

Hensmans, M. (2003). Social movement organizations: A metaphor for strategic actors in institutional fields. *Organization Studies*, 24, 355–381.

Hinings, C.R. & Greenwood, R. (1988). *The dynamics of strategic change*. Oxford: Basil Blackwell Ltd.

Hoskisson, R., Eden, L., Lau, C., & Wright, M. (2000). Strategy in emerging economies. *Academy of Management Journal*, 43, 249–267.

Karra, N., Tracey, P., & Phillips, N. (2006). Altruism and agency in the family firm: Exploring the role of family, kinship and ethnicity. *Entrepreneurship Theory and Practice*, 30, 862–878.

Khanna, T. & Palepu, K. (2006). Emerging giants: Building world class companies in developing countries. *Harvard Business Review*, 84, 60–69.

Kostova, T., & Zaheer, S. (1999). Organizational legitimacy under conditions of complexity: The case of the multinational enterprise. *Academy of Management Review*, 24, 64–81.

Kostova, T. (1999). Transnational transfer of strategic organizational practices: A contextual perspective. *Academy of Management Review*, 24, 308–324.

Lawrence, T., Winn, M.I., & Jennings, P.D. (2001). The temporal dynamics of institutionalization. *Academy of Management Review*, 26, 624–645.

Lawrence, T.B. & Phillips, N. (2004). From Moby Dick to Free Willy: Macrocultural discourse and institutional entrepreneurship in emerging institutional fields. *Organization*, 11, 689–711.

Lawrence, T.B. & Suddaby, R. (2006). Institutional work. In S. Clegg, C. Hardy, T. Lawrence & W. Nord (eds.), *Handbook of organization studies*, 2nd edn, 215–254. London: Sage.

Lawrence, T.B. (1999). Institutional strategy. *Journal of Management*, 25(2), 161–188.

Lawrence, T.B., Hardy, C., & Phillips, N. (2002). Institutional effects of interorganizational collaboration: The emergence of proto-institutions. *Academy of Management Journal*, 45, 281–290.

Leblebici, H., Salancik, G.R., Copay, A., & King, T. (1991). Institutional change and the transformation of interorganizational fields: An organizational history of the U.S. radio broadcasting industry. *Administrative Science Quarterly*, 36, 333–363.

London, T. & Hart, S. (2004). Reinventing strategies for emerging markets: Beyond the transnational model. *Journal of International Business Studies*, 35, 350–370.

Lounsbury, M. (2002). Institutional transformation and status mobility: The professionalization of the field of finance. *Academy of Management Journal*, 45, 255–266.

Luthans, F. & Ibrayeva, E.S. (2006). Entrepreneurial self-efficacy in central Asian transition economies: Quantitative and qualitative analysis. *Journal of International Business Studies*, 37(1), 92–110.

McMillan, J. & Woodruff, C. (2002). The central role of entrepreneurs in transition economies. *Journal of Economic Perspectives*, 16(3), 153–170.

Maguire, S., Hardy, C., & Lawrence, T.B. (2004). Institutional entrepreneurship in emerging fields: HIV/AIDS treatment advocacy in Canada. *Academy of Management Journal*, 47, 657–679.

Meyer, K. (2001). Institutions, transaction costs, and entry mode choice in Eastern Europe. *Journal of International Business Studies*, 32(2), 357–367.

Morris, M., Davis, D., & Allen, J. (1994). Fostering corporate entrepreneurship: cross-cultural comparisons of the importance of individualism versus collectivism. *Journal of International Business Studies*, 25(1), 65–89.

North, D. (1990). *Institutions, institutional change, and economic performance.* New York: Norton.

Oliver, C. (1991). Strategic responses to institutional processes. *Academy of Management Review*, 16, 145–179.

Wu, J. & Pangarkar, N. (2006). Rising to the global challenge: Strategies for firms in emerging markets. *Long Range Planning*, 39, 295–313.

Peng, M.W. (2000). *Business strategies in transition economies.* Thousand Oaks, CA: Sage.

Peng, M.W. 2001. How entrepreneurs create value in transition economies. *Academy of Management Executive*, 15(1), 95–108.

Peng, M.W. (2002). Toward an institution-based view of business strategy. *Asia Pacific Journal of Management*, 19, 251–267.

Peng, M.W. (2003). Institutional transitions and strategic choices. *Academy of Management Review*, 28(2), 275–296.

Phillips, N., Lawrence, T.B., & Hardy, C. (2000). Interorganizational collaboration and the dynamics of institutional fields. *Journal of Management Studies*, 37, 23–43.

Prahalad, C.K. (2004). *Fortune at the bottom of the pyramid: Eradicating poverty through profits.* Wharton School Publishing.

Sahlin-Andersson, K. (1996). Imitating by editing success: The construction of organizational fields. In B. Czarniawska & G. Sevon (eds.), *Translating organizational change*, 69–92. Berlin: Walter de Gruyter.

Scott, W.R. (1995). *Institutions and organizations: Theory and research.* Thousand Oaks, CA: Sage.

Sewell, W.F. (1992). A theory of structure: duality, agency, and transformation. *The American Journal of Sociology*, 98, 1–29.

Spence, J.T. (1985). Achievement American style: the rewards and costs of individualism. *American Psychologist*, 40(2), 1285–1295.

World Bank. (2002). *World development report; Building institutions for markets.* Washington: World Bank.

Wright, M., Filatotchev, I., Hoskisson, R.E., & Peng, M.W. (2005). Strategy research in emerging economies: Challenging the conventional wisdom. *Journal of Management Studies*, 41(1), 1–33.

Xu, D. & Shenkar, O. (2002). Institutional distance and the multinational enterprise. *Academy of Management Review*, 27(4), 608–618.

Zahra, S.A. (1993). A conceptual model of entrepreneurship as firm behavior: A critique and extension. *Entrepreneurship Theory and Practice*, 17, 5–21.

5 Conclusion

Family firms are ubiquitous and yet unique (Howorth et al., 2010). They are heterogeneous in terms of behavior and performance (Basco, 2013). Yet, the diverse and often complex contexts in which they dwell have been largely overlooked (Gupta et al., 2008).

One of my goals in writing this book was to prompt researchers to look more closely at the contexts (e.g., historical, institutional, spatial, and social) in which family firms dwell—and the ways in which context influences the genesis, development, and continuity of these firms (Wright et al., 2014). This could be an area for much fruitful research.

Because much of the literature has concentrated on family firms in developed economies, I chose to study a firm—Neroli—whose network operates in countries with developing economies. In Chapter 2, we saw how family ties and the altruism exhibited by the founder created strong loyalty and a willingness to go the extra mile for the firm. In other words, the family exhibited the kind of reciprocal and symmetrical altruism that creates competitive advantage in a business.

However, as the company matured, we observed how this symmetrical altruistic behavior began to break down. Certain family members no longer reciprocated the altruism but instead began to exhibit behavior like shirking, free riding, and overconsumption of perks. Thus, we observed that there are limits to altruism particularly as a company grows and matures. These dual sides of altruism call for further research.

The founder of Neroli was able to create a dynamic network of entrepreneurs based on a shared ethnic identity (Chapter 3). By expanding his altruism and trust to these entrepreneurs, he succeeded in fostering a feeling of extended family in this network, in effect creating a quasi-family.

However, we also observed in Chapter 3 that the same forces that enable success can constrain when the network seeks to expand. Members sometimes find it difficult to exploit new market opportunities—for example, to expand into markets outside their ethnicity, to find skilled employees belonging to their own ethnic group, or to terminate non-performing employees. This is an important finding because this "darker side" of networks is often omitted from the entrepreneurship literature; the literature tends to focus instead on the enabling effects of networks as a strategic resource. This darker side of networks constitutes a promising area for future research.

In Chapter 4, we discussed the high degree of institutional uncertainty in emerging markets. To many businesses, this uncertainty constitutes a warning to avoid these markets. To more risk-tolerant entrepreneurs, however, these markets represent exciting opportunities. Building on neo-institutional theory, I have framed this entrepreneurship as a kind of *institutional entrepreneurship.*

The entrepreneur creates an "institutional strategy" to create value from the developing organizational field. We discussed three of these strategies: managing institutional uncertainty, spanning institutional voids, and bridging institutional distance.

We also considered neo-institutional theory—which I believe offers a more balanced view of institutions than earlier forms of institutional theory. It includes both formal and informal institutional processes and focuses on strategic action by purposeful actors. For these reasons, I consider it to provide a better foundation for research in this area.

This book, therefore, has focused on acknowledging and exploring family businesses in developing, emerging, and transitional economies. We examined this phenomenon from three different aspects: institutional theory, agency cost, altruism, and kinship as well as the role of ethnicity in building a successful family business. The results have been synthesized in order to offer a complete picture of what it takes to build and manage an entrepreneurial family business in an emerging market economy.

References

Basco, R. (2013). The family's effect on family firm performance: A model testing the demographic and essence approaches. *Journal of Family Business Strategy,* 4(1), 42–66.

Gupta, V., Levenburg, N., Moore, L., Motwani, J., & Schwarz, T.V. (2008). *Culturally-sensitive models of family business in Germanic Europe.* Hyderabad, India: ICFA University Press.

Howorth, C., Rose, M., Hamilton, E., & Westhead, P. (2010). Family firm diversity and development: An introduction. *International Small Business Journal,* 28(5), 437–451.

Wright, M., Chrisman, J.J., Chua, J.H., & Steier, L.P. (2014). Family enterprise and context. *Entrepreneurship Theory and Practice,* 38(6), 1247–1260.

Index

Printed in the United States
by Baker & Taylor Publisher Services